SMOKE-JUMPER

VOLUME 2

MORE STORIES

"Swede" Troedsson

ISBN: 978-1-59152-353-6

For more information or to order extra copies of this book
call Farcountry Press toll free at (800) 821-3874.

sweetgrassbooks
an imprint of Farcountry Press

Produced by Sweetgrass Books
PO Box 5630, Helena, MT 59604; (800) 821-3874;
www.sweetgrassbooks.com

Produced and printed in the United States of America.

30 29 28 27 26 4 5 6 7 8

Dedicated to the memory of
Montana Game Warden

MIKE MEHN

1956–2023

IN MEMORY OF MICHAEL MEHN

August 7, 1956–October 19, 2023
Age 67 of Cascade

MICHAEL DUANE MEHN PASSED AWAY AT HOME with his wife Teri, near Cascade, MT, of natural causes on Thursday, October 19. Mike was born August 7, 1956 in Beaver Dam, WI to Duane and Carleen Mehn. He was the second of four children. His father was a college athletic director and coach, and the family moved a number of times before settling in Mountain Green, UT. After he graduated high school in 1974 he began attending Montana State University (Go Bobcats).

While working on a ranch in the summer near Gardiner, MT, he met his future wife and best friend Teri jo Todd. They wed in June 11, 1977. Mike and Teri had their first son Zakary Scott Mehn on May 9, 1979. After Mike graduated in June, they had their second son Chauncy Duane Mehn on August 2, 1982.

Mike got his dream job as a Montana Fish, Wildlife & Parks Game Warden in 1983 and they moved to his first assignment in Glascow, MT. From there the family moved to Libby,

MT in 1987 and then to his last job as a Game Warden was in Dillon, MT in 1994. Mike and Teri moved to St. George, UT in 2002. They returned to Montana in 2003 after the death of their son Zakary. Mike returned to Fish, Wildlife and Parks where he worked until retiring in 2010 after 27 years with the department. He spent the next 13 years as a licensed contractor, federal court security officer, handyman, and snowbird.

Mike's wife and children couldn't have asked for a better husband and father. He doted on them and always made sure they had everything they needed and knew that he loved them. He always put everyone else before himself, even strangers. Mike was serious about work but often shared his great sense of humor while doing it. He loved the outdoors, the Green Bay Packers, and college football. He enjoyed his family and friends.

Mike was preceded in death by his father Duane, mother Carleen, son Zachary, and granddaughter Tylan. He is survived by his wife Teri, the love of his life, son Chauncey and his wife Aleen (Munday), and children Brecken, Laith, Rynan, Maera and Taison; his brothers Bill and Jack and sister Jill, and numerous cousins, nieces, and nephews. All who knew him adored him.

A well-attended funeral service and reception was held Saturday, October 28, 2023, in Helena, MT.

CONTENTS

AUTHOR'S PREFACE

WHAT FOLLOWS ARE STORIES of my true-life experiences following my high school days.

Stories in this second edition are in addition to the stories that appear in the first edition. They were submitted to the local *Dillonite Daily,* which published my pieces when they could accommodate them.

Many folks who have read them have encouraged me to include them in a second edition.

Credibility of the stories was established by having them reviewed by those who participated in the stories and still survive and can be contacted.

Acknowledgments

A special thanks to Dr. Jack Kirkley, Ph.D., Carol Singer, and Debbie Sporich (owner of The Bookstore in Dillon, Montana), who edited many of my stories and offered suggestions for improvement.

The following participated in, reviewed, and/or contributed to my stories:

- Former smokejumper Rondey Lay
- Retired USDA Forest Service officers Frank Fowler, Mark Petroni, Roger Siemens, and Wayne Smetanka
- Retired Forest Service employees Don Rice and Jim Freestone
- Archaeologist Shannon Gilbert
- Former Beaverhead County Sheriff Rick Later
- Retired rancher Poncho McCoy
- Attorney Karin Troedsson
- Eric Troedsson
- Retired attorney Duke Gilbert III

- Retired Bureau of Land Management employee Pat Fossee
- MT DNRC employee Don Copple
- Billy Pierce; Ernie Christiansen
- MFWP Wildlife Investigator Chad Murphy
- Julie Gobin
- Ann Haggett
- Eleanor Danesh
- and Marie Holt, RN

Sources of Information:

- USDA Forest Service Hank Williams, Jr., rescue case folder.
- National Smokejumper Association Website Links: Jump List, Smokejumper Records, R-1 & R-3 National Smokejumper Association Website, Magazine Link, Jan. 2006 Issue. "Tragedy at Moose Creek," pp. 15–17. April 2021 Issue of *Smokejumper* magazine—photo of Doug Bell.
- Montana Court Record: *State v. Steve Logan* ("Three Shots for a Dime").
- Google: Owyhee Reservoir Web Page.
- *Montana Standard:* March 16, 1995 (–"Too Fat To Fly," p. 1) & December 29, 1995 ("Well War," p. 1).
- U.S. Forest Service case folder, Divide Cabin—photos.
- 8/21/99 Thank you card from Holland ("Dutch Treat").
- Photo, London Bridge & Wayne Fitzwater's Headstone ("London Bridge").
- U.S.M.C. DD-214 ("Record of Service").
- Incident Action Plans, June 1996, South Temperance River Fire ("Artists").
- National Park Service: *Lewis & Clark Journals,* May 31, 1805 (Eye of the Needle) https://lewisandclarkjournals.unl.edu
- Richard McCrea—Yarnell Fire, Lessons Learned

Fire Lookout Tower. PHOTO COURTESY CHRISTOPHER FOELKER, USDA FOREST SERVICE

Chapter One

FIRST SEASON WITH THE USDA FOREST SERVICE

No Smokes

IN THE SUMMER OF 1953, following my first year as a forestry student at Louisiana State University, I accepted a job as a fire lookout on the Superior Ranger District on the Lolo National Forest, Montana. I hitchhiked from Baton Rouge, LA, to Superior, Montana.

I was packed into the Marble Mountain Lookout, situated south of the Clark Fork River, between Superior and St. Regis, Montana.

I was on the lookout for six weeks, and although 1953 was a busy fire season, I never spotted a fire. One day, Hank Vische, the district fire dispatcher, called me on the phone and, after giving the directions to a fire, asked me if I could see the smoke. I was not provided binoculars, and I told him I could not see the smoke. He sounded agitated that I could not see the smoke. He kept asking me if I was sure. I kept replying, "NO, I CAN'T SEE THE SMOKE!"

A couple of years later, I was finishing my tour in the Marines. At Camp Pendleton, California, a buddy of mine and I were watching a hawk hovering above us (looking for a mouse or vole, I suppose).

My buddy's glasses fell off. I picked them up, and out of curiosity, put them on and looked up at the hawk. WOW! I realized then and there I must be nearsighted. The corpsman at sick bay confirmed my suspicions. He said,

"Private, you are DEFINITELY nearsighted!" A Navy optometrist prescribed corrective lenses.

Now I know why at the rifle range the 500-yard target appeared fuzzy. In spite of that I did qualify as a sharpshooter, sending rounds downrange in the target's general direction. I think with corrective lenses I may have qualified as expert.

This also may explain why I never spotted a fire while on lookout. A nearsighted lookout with no binoculars! SHEESH!

However, I had a great time on lookout! I sunned myself on the shutters, baked pies, tried the recipes listed in the great *Lookout Cookbook,* watched a bull elk and a black bear who routinely wandered around my lookout, and gossiped on the phone in the evening with other lookouts.

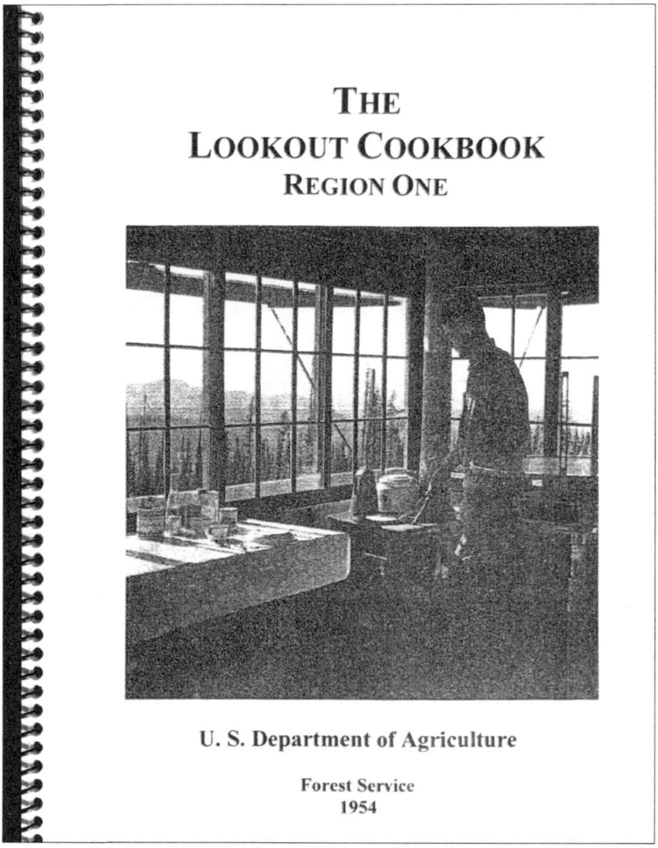

Chapter Two

U.S. MARINE CORPS EXPERIENCES

Age Limit

DURING THE PERIOD FROM 1954 TO 1956, I served in the Marines. One of the Marines in my company was Dick Zahn. Dick was a farm boy from Aberdeen, South Dakota. Dick related to us how he found out there was an age limit as to when he could be served a beer.

Dick went on to tell us that when he was ten years old, he would help his family put up hay. At noon the women would come into the fields with lunch and buckets of cold beer. Being a hard-working member of the hay crew, Dick was entitled to drink the beer.

One HOT summer day, during a break between hay cuttings, the family spent the day shopping in Aberdeen. As Dick was roaming around town, he developed a terrible thirst. As he was passing by the entrance to a saloon, he could smell the aroma of beer.

Dick walked into the saloon. The bartender was alone, putting the shine on some glasses, with his back to Dick. Dick walked up to the bar, looked up, and ordered a beer. The bartender turned around to see where this voice was coming from. He then looked down over the top of the bar and saw this young boy looking up at him. The bartender then informed Dick he was too young to be served alcohol.

Flop House

In March 1955, after returning from Korea, I was stationed at the Camp Pendleton Marine Corps Base.

Later that year I decided to spend a weekend of liberty in Los Angeles. I purchased a round-trip bus ticket in Oceanside and arrived in Los Angeles in time to attend a dance and party at a local dance pavilion. Towards the end of a wild evening, I was hit on by a gorgeous woman. By then I was broke and could not afford to entertain her. All I had was the round-trip bus ticket and no way to pay for lodging.

I had heard of a local church that ran a hostel that would take in those who were down and out. Upon checking in, I was issued a little cloth sack into which to place my valuables and instructed to pin in it to my skivvies (underpants) so as to prevent theft during the night. In the sleeping room I was assigned a top bunk, and I slept the night.

The next morning I participated in singing a religious song in order to qualify for the free breakfast. Following breakfast, I boarded a bus and returned to Camp Pendleton.

AWOL

I served as a Marine for two years in the Active Duty Reserve Program during the period from 1954 to1956. I was assigned to H&S Company, 3rd Battalion, 7th Regiment, 1st Marine Division.

On our return from Korea, we were stationed at Camp Pendleton, California. Our battalion commander was Colonel Michner, a harsh and hated commander. He was quick to subject a Marine who had committed a minor infraction of a regulation to a special court-martial, rather than to a summary court-martial. The potential penalty resulting from a conviction in a special court-Martial was a lot harsher than the potential penalty in a summary court-martial. Also, many Marines were having their weekend pass canceled for frivolous reasons.

One Monday morning, our weekly Battalion Report listed thirty-five Marines AWOL (Absent Without Leave), thirty incarcerated in the brig, and five listed as deserters (AWOL exceeding thirty days).

The next day, following an investigation by an investigative board comprised of generals, Colonel Michner was relieved of his command. He was replaced by Major Mitchell Paige. Many of our officers exhibited service and campaign ribbons that were earned in WWII or Korea on their chests. Major Paige exhibited just one. It was pale blue with white stars. It recognized him as having earned the Medal of Honor for his actions in WWII. (His impressive citation can be viewed on the Congressional Medal of Honor Society website.)

Major Paige immediately pardoned many of the Marines in the brig. Among those pardoned was a good buddy of mine. He had gone AWOL and joined a carnival in Oregon. His plan was to return before the end of thirty days to avoid being charged with desertion. He failed to take into account that the month he was AWOL was thirty-one days long! He was found guilty of desertion in a special court-martial.

I was issued a .45 pistol and ordered to go to the brig and bring my buddy back to the company. When my buddy appeared at the brig gate, he wanted to know what I was doing there. I informed him I was there to return his sorry ass back to our company. He'd been pardoned!

Formation

In the latter part of 1955, just prior to my discharge from active duty in the U.S. Marine Corps, I returned from a weekend of liberty in San Francisco. I finally got into bed in my barracks in Camp Pendleton at 2:00 a.m. on Monday morning. Reveille was at 0600. We were to get up and assemble on the parade ground shortly thereafter.

Many of us had returned from a wild weekend from wherever. So we staggered out onto the parade ground in a less than happy mood. Many of us, having just returned from Korea, were "short-timers" with little service time left. We were a pretty grumpy and "salty" bunch there at O-dark thirty.

The weekend duty officer was a brand-new second lieutenant. There he proudly stood, under the parade ground streetlight, his new gold shoulder bars glinting as he waited to call us to attention.

The moment had arrived, and he shouted the preparatory command "BATTALION!" to call us to attention. There was a pause as the command was repeated by the company commanders: "COMPANY!" And then, from the platoon commanders: "TOON!"

But, before he could give the attention command, somewhere from the rear of our formation came the agonizing shout: "WHAAAT!" Giggles of laughter rippled across the ranks! The duty officer went ballistic. He demanded to know who said that. After receiving no response, he ordered that we were to run ten laps around the parade ground.

The formation made only half a lap and disintegrated as all of us Marines charged back to our barracks. The duty officer was left standing alone on the parade ground knowing that he commanded very little respect from these men.

Hooch

In early 1956 I finished my two-year reserve active duty service in the U.S. Marine Corps. Following my return from Korea in 1955, my remaining active duty was spent in Camp Las Pulgas, a division of Camp Pendleton, California.

During the latter part of 1955, it was observed that some of the Marines on KP (Kitchen Police) mess man duty were sloshed while serving food in the chow line. Commanding officers were puzzled as to the source of the booze. Liquor was prohibited among the enlisted men on the base. The men would not reveal the source.

In the commanding officers' desperation to find the source of the liquor, they ordered all vehicles entering the base to be searched by Military Police. The vehicle searches revealed nothing.

One day one of the cooks was looking for a clean garbage can in the steam room. The steam room was located at the rear of the mess hall. He needed a clean garbage can to store some dry food items. His gaze fell on a garbage can that had its lid firmly attached. To satisfy his curiosity, and with some effort, he finally removed the lid, whereupon fermenting raisins shot up and stuck to the ceiling! The cook dipped a forefinger into the brew, liked what he tasted, and said nothing.

Sometime later a civilian employee discovered the still and reported it.

Later I heard that the still was relocated to the top of the flat mess hall roof.

Chapter Three

A SEASON ON THE SKYKOMISH DISTRICT

Yellow Jackets

IN 1957 I was employed as a timber aide for the summer on the Skykomish Ranger District in Washington.

I was part of a four-man crew preparing a large timber sale. We were camped in the proposed timber sale area. The forest floor was dry from lack of recent rains. Every day we would stumble into yellow jacket nests.

One day, Forester Bob Norton and I were chaining out (measuring) section lines to find section and quarter corners. We would sign the corners in order to protect them during road construction and logging operations. Using the recorded distances between the corners, we would use a two-chain (132-foot) metal measuring tape to find the corners. Bob was the lead chainman, following his compass and walking along the section line between corners.

I was the rear chainman. When Bob would reach the end of two chains, I could feel a brass tab at the end of the chain sliding through my hand. This would indicate to me that he had progressed two chains, and I would stop him by shouting out "CHAIN!" Bob would stop so I could walk up to his location in order to start the next two-chain measurement.

During one of the measurements, I could feel the chain start to accelerate thorough my hand. The brass tab zipped through my grip, and the end of the chain disappeared. I kept shouting "CHAIN! CHAIN!" so Bob would stop.

Caulked boots worn by foresters working in the coastal timber (ten-inch tops, spring heels).
(Size 0 caulks and triconi edge nails)

The next time I saw Bob he was upslope above me, hopping, shouting, and frantically beating on his leg with his hard hat, while still holding onto the chain. A yellow jacket was crawling up his leg inside his pant leg. He was attempting to kill it before it reached more sensitive areas.

After killing the yellow jacket before harm was done, Bob joined me, still dragging the chain. I was sitting down and laughing so hard tears were rolling down my cheeks.

One of our crew, Jim Reynolds, was very allergic to bee stings. To avoid a medical crisis, Jim was dismissed from the cruise camp and sent back to the ranger station.

1987, Cruise Camp, Maloney Mtn. *Left to right:* "Swede" Johnson, "Swede" Troedsson, and Jim Reynolds. PHOTO COURTESY BOB NORTON

1958, First Training Jump.
I smokejumped out of Missoula, Montana, during the 1958 & 1959 fire seasons

Chapter Four

SMOKEJUMPER EXPERIENCES

Doug Bell* [1] *(MSO-1958)

IN THE APRIL 2021 ISSUE OF *SMOKEJUMPER* MAGAZINE, I noticed a photo of Doug Bell in front of his car. This brought back fond memories of Doug Bell.

eaded home after 1958 season. L-R: Tom Greiner (MSO-55), Doug Bell (MSO-58). Note custo
ck, high-mileage replacement tires, and crates of rat-holed C-Rations to help get through the fall se

[1] The designation and year denotes the smokejumper base and year trained. MSO is Missoula.

In 1958, at the Missoula Smokejumper Base, I trained with Doug. Doug was (ahem) a unique individual from Oklahoma. He had a two-door coup on which he fashioned a custom top luggage rack.

The rack was constructed of two-by-fours bolted to the side of the car. Additional two-by-fours completed the rack. In the rack were several well-worn spare tires, and some "rat-holed" C-rations to sustain him on his weekend ventures.

On weekends when he was not jumping on fires, Doug would quite often motor up to Glacier National Park to chase the gorgeous female summer employees. On Saturday nights the park would host a dance at their main hotel. Sometimes the car would break down, so Doug would have to bum a ride back to the disabled car with a repair part.

Doug wore bib overalls. In his shirt pocket he carried a pet white-footed deer mouse. Sometimes, when in conversation with Doug, the mouse would stick its nose out of his pocket, look around, and after a few twitches of its whiskers, it would retreat back into Doug's pocket.

Doug was always full of entertaining conversation. One morning at the breakfast table Doug was silent. When questioned why he was quiet, Doug sadly replied that during his sleep the previous night he rolled over the mouse, killing it.

Frenchy

In early September 1959, as fire activity wound down, smokejumpers would be assigned to ranger districts to clear trails, roll up telephone wire, and assist in other duties. The smokejumper project would pay the jumpers' wages, and the districts would receive labor for room and board. It was a win-win arrangement.

Four of us jumpers were assigned to the Ford Work Center on the Flathead National Forest. Ford is located on the North Fork of the Flathead River, about ten miles north of Polebridge, Montana. Ford and the Ford Work Center are located across the river from Glacier National Park (GNP). Our assignment was to assist an engineering survey crew.

The work center had a cook named Frenchy. Frenchy was a fantastic cook, but had an addiction to alcohol. Frenchy was aware that if he went to town on the weekend, chances were he would not return to Ford in time to prepare breakfast Monday morning.

In order for Frenchy to be on pay status at Ford over the weekend, he was required to cook for at least six men at Ford.

At dinner Friday evening, Frenchy would post the weekend menu. Steaks, prime rib roast, ham, pies, homemade rolls, and all kinds of goodies. The temptation usually worked!

We were presented a terrible dilemma. Here we were, four jumpers with enormous appetites for home cooking and a high level of testosterone. Do we stay at Ford to partake of Frenchy's fantastic cuisine, or do we attend the Saturday night dance at the Glacier Hotel in Glacier National Park? Among the summer employees were gorgeous women from France, Germany, and Scandinavia. They would be at the dance!

One of our crew met a beautiful German woman at one of the Saturday night dances. Her first name was Hergart. He nicknamed her "Huggy," and he eventually married her!

Wheels Off

I noticed Rondey Lay's (MSO-67) name in a quarterly issue of *Smokejumper* magazine. It brought back a fond memory of Rondey.

In 1996 I attended Rondey's retirement party held on his ranch near Florence, Montana. His party was combined with the end of the jump season termination party. Rondey had jumped for fifteen seasons. Prior to retiring he was working in the warehouse at the Aerial Fire Depot, servicing chain saws and pumps. To say he was a legend was an understatement!

I was impressed with one of Rondey's uses of his mules and wagon. His favorite elk hunting area was at the head of a drainage on the east side of the Bitterroot Valley. It was a haven for elk. Motorized access into the area was blocked by a Forest Service–locked gate.

During the start of the hunting season, Rondey would hitch up his mules to his wagon and proceed to the gate. Upon arriving at the gate, he would unhitch the mules and remove the wagon wheels. Then he would walk the mules around the gate and have them drag the wagon bed UNDER the gate. After replacing the wheels, he would load up his camp, grub, and various nectars onto the wagon. Then he and his buddies would proceed to the head of the drainage, set up camp, cook steaks, drink beer and whiskey, tell jump stories, and kill elk.

Rondey is alive and well at the time of this writing. He sold his ranch in Florence, and lives on his brother's ranch in Ryegate, Montana.

Pay Disparity

During the period from 8/6/45 to 6/3/21, forty-four smokejumpers were killed in the line of duty. The "Killed In The Line of Duty" link in the National Smokejumper Association website lists those killed, input about them from those who knew the jumper, and the cause of death:

CAUSES OF DEATH:	
Letdown	2
Falling Snag	2
Plane Crash	5
Helicopter Crash	1
Landing	3
Drowning	1
Strangled	2
Broken Neck	1
Fire	26
Parachuting	1
Total	44

As of 2021, starting pay for a new wildland firefighter for the California Department of Forestry and Fire Protection (CAL FIRE) was $29/hr. Experienced firefighters for CAL FIRE received $42.24/hr. Starting pay in 2021 for a smokejumper was $16/hr. On 12/28/21, starting pay for a McDonald's restaurant employee in Bozeman was advertised at $20/hr.

Final Request

On August 3rd, 1959, eight of us smokejumpers jumped the Fawn Ridge Fire above the Salmon River in Idaho. The next day, after declaring the fire out, we hiked down to Lanz Bar and were transported upriver by jet boat to the Corn Creek boat ramp. We spent the night at the Salmon River Ranger Station. The next morning we boarded a Johnson Flying Service DC-3 at the Salmon Airport for the flight back to Missoula.

On the flight to Missoula, the word was passed throughout the cabin that two jumpers died the previous day in a fiery Ford Trimotor plane crash in Moose Creek, Idaho. One of the jumpers was Gary Williams (MSO-59), a good buddy and classmate of mine. Gary and I had trained together that year. The news brought tears to my eyes.

Shortly thereafter Gary's fiancé came out to the Missoula Smokejumper Base to look me up. She wanted to know how Gary died. I took her by the hand and led her into an unoccupied room in the dorm. Struggling to keep my composure, I gently related the circumstances that led to Gary's death.

When that devastated woman left, I wondered what the future held for her.

I found out later that Gary had been sitting in the cabin under the aircraft wing. When the plane crashed, gasoline from the wing fuel tank poured over Gary and ignited. Gary, critically burned, dashed out of the plane and collapsed on the ground. Two jumpers, Roland Pera (MSO-56) and Bob Reid (MSO-57), had hiked into Moose Creek earlier that morning off a two-man fire and were waiting to be flown to Missoula. They witnessed the crash and ran over to John Rolf (MS0-57) and Gary, who were both critically burned, to render aid and comfort. Gary died about an hour after the crash. John, who was still lucid, knew that Roland had a beautiful singing voice, and asked Roland to sing to him. It was John's final request. He died in Grangeville, Idaho, that night.

Eventually, Gary's former fiancé married a college classmate and good friend of mine. I was elated.

I had the pleasure of being invited to their fiftieth wedding anniversary celebration at the Chico Hot Springs Resort in Pray, Montana.

Roger Siemens (MSO-1959)

The PBS TV documentary about the 1961 Higgins Ridge Fire in Idaho prompted me to write about Roger Siemens.

Roger and I trained together in 1959 in Missoula as smokejumpers. He went on to jump for four seasons. He was one of the twenty jumpers to be rescued by helicopter from the Higgins Ridge Fire. He told me his first ride on a helicopter was in the cargo rack of that helicopter!

Roger was a native of Iowa and graduated with a degree in wildlife biology from Missoula.

His career with the USDA Forest Service included positions on the Custer, Bitterroot, Gallatin, and Deerlodge National Forests. Following a period as the district ranger on the Jefferson Ranger District, Roger retired in 1994 as the recreation specialist on the Beaverhead National Forest. He and his wife Rita resided in Silver Star, Montana, after his retirement.

As a retiree, Roger and his wife owned R&R Resources. They would assist local ranchers on predator and rattlesnake control. He loved to hunt coyotes and was an expert at handling rattlesnakes. He was also very enthusiastic about sharing his knowledge about snakes with others, and frequently visited school classrooms and other organizations to present his live rattlesnake demonstration.

The University of Montana Western Environmental Science Department would host guest speakers throughout the school year for their "On The Rocks" program. I suggested they invite Roger to give his rattlesnake presentation, and the faculty finally accepted my suggestion.

Using his rattlesnakes, Roger gave a fascinating program to a packed audience in the largest lecture room in Block Hall. He asked me to fill a plastic bag inside a leather purse with hot water. Dangling the warm object in front of the snake prompted the snake to strike at the bag, demonstrating how heat-sensitive pits helped it aim its strikes.

I mentioned to Roger that I wondered what the audience reaction would be if at the conclusion of his program, as he was packing up his snakes, he would look around with a worried look on his face and mention that he was missing Charlie, his most short-tempered snake. He grinned and said he was not going there.

Roger died in December 2021 of a heart attack while he was hunting coyotes. He was eighty-two years old.

The Ford could transport 8 smokejumpers & spotter; the DC-2 12 smokejumpers & spotter; the DC-3 16 & Spotter; the Twin Beech 4 Smokejumpers & Spotter; and the Travel Air 2 smokejumpers & Spotter.

JOHNSON FLYING SERVICE AIRCRAFT

Ford Trimotor. (Grangeville '59) PHOTO COURTESY BILL KOLAR

DC-2 & 3. (Missoula '57). PHOTO COURTESY ROGER SAVAGE

Twin Beech. (Missoula '57) PHOTO COURTESY ROGER SAVAGE

Travel Air. (Missoula '64) PHOTO COURTESY DICK HUGHES

Chapter Five

NPRR FORESTER

The Wrong Bed

IN THE SUMMER OF 1960, three of us foresters hired on with the Northern Pacific Railroad to participate in their timber sale program in the Seeley/Swan Valley in Montana.

Towards the end of the summer we moved from Seeley Lake into a cabin rented from Ed Underwood. Ed was a local building contractor. The rental cabin was about five miles south of Condon, Montana.

Shortly after we moved into Ed's rental cabin, he informed us that he recently had to testify at a murder trial in the Missoula County Courthouse. Ed went on to explain that a Swedish immigrant named Lundborg and his wife lived about a mile down the road from Ed's home.

One day Lundborg realized that he forgot his lunch bucket. Upon returning to his home, he observed a strange truck in his yard. When he entered his home he found a stranger in bed with his wife. Lundborg, standing at the bedroom entrance, ordered the man out. The man put on his trousers and squeezed by Lundborg on his way out.

A short time later, suspecting that the affair was still ongoing, Lundborg returned to his home to find the same pickup truck parked in his front yard. Lundborg called the man out. The man grabbed a .22-caliber rifle off of Lundborg's living room wall, and upon exiting the house, told Lundborg to stick his head up and he would shoot it off. So Lundborg stuck his head up—and shot and killed his wife's lover with his .30-.40 Krag rifle.

Immediately after the shooting, Lundborg's wife, fearing for her life, ran up to Ed's home to report the shooting and to seek shelter.

At trial Lundborg's defense attorney asked Lundborg what he said to the stranger as the stranger squeezed his way by him on his way out of Lundborg's bedroom. In a heavy Swedish accent, Lundborg replied that he had said, "By golly, one of these days you're going to go too far!"

The packed courtroom burst into laughter. It took the judge a minute or so to gavel the courtroom spectators back into silence.

At trial Lundborg had two things going for him in his defense. The stranger had threatened Lundborg with deadly force, hence the shooting could be justified as self defense. Also, Lundborg's wife had filed for a divorce which was effective at noon the day of the shooting. Lundborg shot his wife's lover at 11:00 a.m. that day. Lundborg's wife was still his wife. Lundborg was acquitted of murder.

The next year I ended my employment with the railroad. When I left the Swan Valley, Lundborg was still hunting elk with that .30-,40 Krag rifle.

GREEN MOUNTAIN BEARPAWS

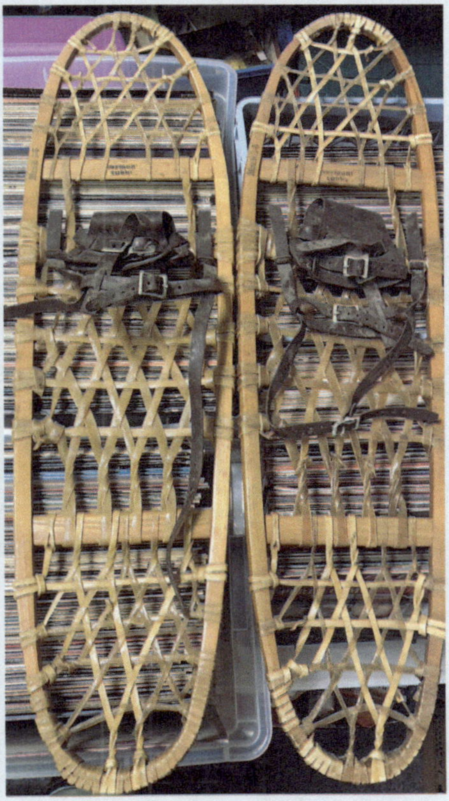

Snowshoes were the mode of transportation in the timber from January to March

Chapter Six

FOREST SERVICE EXPERIENCES

I WAS EMPLOYED BY THE USDA FOREST SERVICE from June 1961 until May 1994. During my first two years, I was stationed on the Curlew Ranger District on the Colville National Forest in northeastern Washington. The balance of my career was spent on the Beaverhead National Forest in southwest Montana.

Louie Somday

From 1961 to1963 I was stationed on the Curlew Ranger District on the Colville National Forest in Washington. Curlew is located north of Spokane, and is also about twenty-five miles north of the Colville Indian Reservation.

The Colville Indians love their horses. Near Curlew lived an elderly Colville Indian named Louie Somday. Louie had numerous horses. He would often walk out into his horse pasture and stand among his horses just to admire them.

One day a rancher, who was Louie's neighbor, came into the ranger station to complain that Louie's horses were trespassing onto his ranch. The ranger informed the rancher that we could not do anything about Louie's horses until they were on national forest land.

As the rancher was leaving our office, he was heard muttering, "I think Louie's horses are headed that way."

A week later the rancher returned to our ranger station and informed us that Louie's horses were now on national forest land. After confirming the location of Louie's horses, he was ordered to remove the horses from the national forest. He made no effort to remove his horses, so eventually we rounded up and impounded his horses.

After reimbursing the government for the roundup and impoundment costs, Louie's horses were returned to him.

Toasted Peacocks

In 1962, while stationed on the Curlew Ranger District, there was a farm across the highway from the ranger station on which there were peacocks.

One morning, two of the peacocks roosted on the cross arms of a nearby power pole. During the course of their antics, I suspect they must have touched and completed a circuit. As I was about to leave for the field, I heard an explosion and saw a bright blue flash and a puff of smoke! The result: two toasted peacocks lying at the base of the power pole, a blown transformer, and our ranger station and the nearby town of Curlew without power for the rest of the day.

Big Brown

In 1968 I supervised a crew of eight temporary Forest Service summer employees. We were tasked with establishing, measuring, and recording sample timber plots on Beaverhead National Forest lands in the Madison Valley in Montana.

One day one of my crew and I were eating our lunch at the West Fork Madison River Rest Area, just downriver from the recently constructed Lyon Bridge, about thirty-five miles south of Ennis. While eating our lunch, a vehicle with California license plates arrived and parked at the rest area. An elderly woman and a boy, who appeared to be about ten years old, exited the vehicle. The boy began to assemble a fishing pole. I approached the boy and suggested he walk out onto the bridge and drop a baited hook into a large hole that had developed in the Madison River bottom, just downstream below the center bridge column. I mentioned to him that workers constructing the bridge had pulled some huge fish from this hole. The boy finished assembling his pole, and after baiting the hook, ran out onto the bridge and dropped the baited hook into the hole.

I had no sooner returned to my vehicle than I heard the boy shouting. Turning around, I could see the boy had hooked into a big fish. His fishing pole was bent way over and he could not lift the fish, which was thrashing in the water twenty feet below him. I shouted and motioned to him to hang onto his catch and run to the end of the bridge and down to the river's edge. Upon arriving at the river's edge, the boy was able to land what appeared to be an eight-pound brown trout!

It turned out the elderly woman was the boy's grandmother. I offered to take a photo of her with her grandson and the big fish, using her camera.

The grandmother thanked me profusely for facilitating her grandson's success. They planned to share the fish with relatives in Ennis with whom they were staying. They had quite a story to tell when they returned to California!

340 Weatherby

For most of my career I was stationed in the Beaverhead National Forest supervisor's office in Dillon, Montana.

During the latter part of the 1980s, just prior to the opening of the general hunting season, a husky Wisconsin logger would often visit me in the office to discuss guns and hunting opportunities. He would often say, "Would you speak up, please?"

I suspect his decline in hearing was due to operating chain saws and heavy logging equipment most of his life.

The last time he visited me he stated that in the previous year he had been hunting elk in the Notch, located in the Snowcrest Range Mountains south of Dillon. He went on to state that he had been using a .300 Weatherby Magnum rifle. Because of the long shots, he felt the need for something more powerful.

Just prior to leaving home for his trip to Montana, he purchased a MORE POWERFUL and EXREMELY LOUD .340 Weatherby Magnum rifle. In the course of sighting it in, he shot a whole box (twenty rounds) of ammunition.

I exclaimed, "Good Lord, I hope you were wearing hearing protection!"

He responded, "Would you speak up, please?"

Artifacts

In August 1967, I was dispatched to a fire on the Bonners Ferry Ranger District in northern Idaho.

My assignment was as a Crew Boss supervising a crew of approximately twenty-one Pueblo Indians from Arizona.

Our sector straddled Bugle Creek, a deep draw with steep banks. There were three pump emplacements in the draw, one of which presented a difficult climb in order to get up onto the hose line.

The first day I had the crew, they disappeared for a while and returned with a log into which they had chopped steps so that they could more easily ascend the steep bank above the one pump emplacement.

I called the Crew Boss over and expressed my admiration of their ladder. The Crew Boss said this was the method they used in Arizona to climb up into their pueblos.

I also instructed the Crew Boss that when they were done using their makeshift ladder they should chop it into small pieces and scatter it over the land. My concern was that an archaeologist might later discover this Pueblo artifact in northern Idaho and get historians excited over his discovery!

Later, while we were taking a break, we saw a beautiful weasel-like animal cross our fire line. The weasel was about the size of a large cat. It had brown fur with a rust hue and black legs. None of us knew what kind of weasel this critter was.

When I arrived back home, I looked up the weasel and determined it was a fisher. I notified the Bonners Ferry Ranger District of our sighting. They informed me they had planted some fishers in the area for porcupine control.

Beavers

In early July 1988, I was dispatched to Duluth, Minnesota, to advise the Superior National Forest in managing their aviation activities. The forest was experiencing numerous fires.

The Superior National Forest is the only forest in the National Forest System that has De Haviland Beaver aircraft. The forest, in 1988, had three of these beautiful, single-engine aircraft. In the summer they were on floats.

De Haviland Beaver. PHOTO COURTSEY US FOREST SERVICE

These aircraft had a seventy-gallon tank into which they could scoop water to drop on fires. In the winter one aircraft was placed on skis in order to patrol the Boundary Waters Canoe Wilderness Area to detect Canadian and American snowmobilers operating illegally in the wilderness area. These aircraft were based in Ely, Minnesota.

To get a handle on this aviation program, I spent several days in Ely so I could fly with each of the pilots.

One day while I was a passenger in one of the Beavers, the pilot got a radio call notifying him of a nearby fire. The pilot informed me that he could not scoop up water with me on board. He would drop me off at a nearby lake and return to pick me up when he was finished dropping water.

We arrived over a lake that was ringed with summer cabins. I asked the pilot to check to see if there was a party going on at one of the cabins. It was too early in the season for parties. The pilot landed and taxied up to the shore. I jumped from a float onto the shore, and the pilot departed to perform his water drops.

A gentleman came down from one of the cabins carrying a HUGE glass filled with an alcoholic drink. He appeared well sloshed. He offered me a drink. I denied his offer because I was on official duty. I informed him I'd be happy to accept a soda pop. He brought me a Pepsi, and we sat and visited while the pilot was dropping water. After about half an hour, the pilot returned and taxied up to the lake shore. I thanked the gentleman for the Pepsi, jumped onto the float, climbed into the aircraft cabin, and departed from the lake.

NOTAM

In 1994 I was dispatched to the Moose Creek Ranger Station, located in the Selway-Bitterroot Wilderness Area in Idaho. My assignment was to supervise the TFR (Temporary Flight Restriction) surrounding the ranger station. This TFR, which had been filed with the FAA by District Ranger Barry Hicks, restricted the air space around the ranger station. This was necessary because of the busy fire suppression activity in the area.

Moose Creek Ranger Station has an airfield for logistical support. It also serves as a fly-in facility for pilots wishing to stay at the nearby campground and fish the Lochsa River.

When I deplaned at Moose Creek there were already some private aircraft parked at the airfield. They had arrived prior to the TFR being activated. The campers were allowed to continue their stay, but once they left, they could not return while the TFR was active.

The morning after I arrived, a Cessna 170 landed at Moose Creek early in the morning. The pilot and his passenger deplaned and began to assemble their fishing poles. I walked over to the pilot and asked him if he had checked the NOTAMs (Notice to Airmen) before departing home to see if there was a TFR on the Moose Creek airfield. He stated he had not. I then informed him he was in violation of the TFR and suggested he and his passenger depart the area. With a sly smile, he said that the temperature had gotten too warm to safely take off. I suggested we check his aircraft performance charts. He stated he did not have them with him. I suspect he was beginning to realize that he was confronted by someone with pilot experience. (I had taken the FAA private pilot training and became a certified pilot.)

I then informed the pilot that I would not put him in danger. I told him that he and his passenger were NOT going fishing, but that they could sit in the shade of a wing until the temperature cooled enough in the evening so he could safely depart Moose Creek. He was welcome to use our toilet facilities, and we would deliver sack lunches and water.

I was returning to my radio desk when I heard the Cessna start up. The pilot and his passenger took off and departed the area. I suspect spending the day sitting in the shade of a wing did not appeal to him!

Palm Trees

In 1994 I was assigned to a wildland fire near the Clearwater Junction, about forty miles east of Missoula, Montana. My assignment was to supervise helicopter operations.

One of the helicopters on our fire was a Kaman helicopter. This efficient heavy lift helicopter was being used in water bucket operations. Earlier models of this helicopter had a stubby fuselage and twin rotors mounted side-by-side. It was fascinating to watch the intertwined blades rotate without contacting each other.

One day I was visiting with the helicopter pilot while he was shut down for fuel. He informed me that he had come from a logging operation in South Carolina. Every morning while on the logging operation a local farmer would arrive, with his thumbs hooked into his bib overalls suspenders, and stand nearby to watch the helicopter operate.

South Carolina State Flag

The farmer walked over to the pilot one morning while the pilot was preparing for the day's operation and told the pilot that the helicopter looked like "two palm trees making love in a dumpster."[1]

Falling Buffalo

There is a historical indigenous buffalo jump next to the Ruby River Road. This buffalo jump is located about one mile north of where the Sweetwater Road joins the Ruby River Road, south of Alder, Montana. The jump location is displayed on the Beaverhead-Deerlodge National Forest South map.

In the 1980s a summer employee on the Sheridan Ranger District constructed an official-looking Montana Highway Department caution sign.

[1] A palmetto tree is displayed on the South Carolina state flag. In 1776 during the Revolutionary War, on Sullivan's Island, South Carolina, troops defending a new fort used palmetto tree logs to successfully deflect cannon balls from the British fleet. The palmetto tree was added to the state flag in 1861.

The sign had a yellow background with the outline and the buffalo shown in black. He installed the sign on the edge of the road, at the base of the buffalo jump. The caution sign displayed a falling buffalo.

The sign lasted about two weeks and then disappeared.

Fire Below

In the 1980s I was assigned as a sector boss on a fire in the Salmon River country in Idaho. I was supervising several fire crews building fire line downhill on a steep slope with fire below them. One of my crew was closest to the fire below. Their Crew Boss recognized the potential threat to his crew and pulled his crew out of my sector. A basic firefighting rule is you NEVER build fire line downhill with fire below you.

That evening in camp, I searched for the Crew Boss. Upon locating him I shook his hand and told him he did the right thing in leaving my sector after recognizing the potential threat to his crew.

A wildland fire researcher stated that 80 percent of wildland fire fatalities involve fire below. The 1949 Mann Gulch Fire, near Helena, Montana, comes to mind. Thirteen firefighters, including twelve smokejumpers, were killed trying to outrun a fire that blew up below them. I read two accounts in the National Smokejumper Association's quarterly magazine where smokejumpers refused orders to build fire line downhill with fire below them. In both instances the fires later blew up and would have killed the smokejumpers had they obeyed the orders.

The House Fuel Model

In 1990 I was dispatched to the Dude Fire, near Payson, Arizona. Prior to my arrival, six firefighters—five prison convicts and their handler—were killed trying to protect a home.

In my opinion, sometimes when a fire threatens homes (the house fuel model), fire overhead (supervisors) establish priorities to save homes. (Wildland firefighters are not trained in structure protection.) Then, sometimes, responding to political pressure, bad decisions are made, and sometimes firefighters die.

In 2013 the Yarnell Hill Fire, near Yarnell, Arizona, killed nineteen firefighters on their way to protect some homes. They were urban structure firefighters who were standing safely in the black (burned over area) when they spotted a fire threatening homes below them. Their structure protection instinct kicked in, and they decided to leave the safety of the black and run downhill to try to save the homes. They never made it.

Antiquities Act

In 2022 I ran into an archaeologist in a local grocery store in Dillon, Montana. In the course of our conversation, I mentioned that I had written a book entitled *Smokejumper & Other Stories.* She seemed interested, so I retrieved a copy from my car and showed it to her. After she purchased the book I showed her a picture of a sarsaparilla bottle displayed in my book. I had found the bottle sixty years ago on the Skykomish Ranger District in Washington, and had it displayed on my mantlepiece.

The archaeologist said I should have left it in place. I smirked and replied that I may have found the bottle before the Antiquities Act was passed.

When I got home I Googled the Antiquities Act and found out it was signed by Teddy Roosevelt in 1906!

A few weeks later I saw the archaeologist in a local brewery. She was sitting with some friends, one of whom was an archaeologist. I showed her the picture of the sarsaparilla bottle in my book. The woman I met at the store muttered, "I'm going to let this one go." I thought, "Oh, boy."

Feeling somewhat guilty, I later described on a map where I found the bottle, packaged up the map and bottle with a cover letter, and delivered the package to the archaeologist. In the letter I stated I was about to downsize, and it was better that she have the bottle rather than it being sent to the landfill.

The archaeologist sent me the sweetest thank you letter in which offered to hire me! She later told me that bottle sits on top of her bookcase in her office, and she thinks of me every time she looks at it.

You got to love that woman!

The Way It Was

Prior to 1980, on wildland fires, there was no fourteen-day duty limitation. Overtime was paid as straight time. There was no hazard pay. There were no catered meals or showers in camp. You just felt fortunate if the fire happened to be close to a lake or river so you could bathe occasionally. You also felt fortunate if you could visit a laundromat en route from one fire to the next.

You had no choice but to accept a dispatch to a fire. One year our Beaverhead National Forest supervisor, Joe Wagenfer, called all of us into the conference room. He told us he was responding to a complaint from the forest dispatcher, who said he was having a hard time filling orders for firefighters because some of our firefighters were refusing to accept fire assignments. Joe bluntly stated: "Folks, there's two buses leaving town. One is going to the fire, the other is going down the road." That stern message pretty well cured the reluctance to accept fire assignments.

Accepting fire assignments took precedence over some personal health and family situations. In 1967 I started the fire season weighing a robust 165 pounds. By the end of the fire season, I weighed a gaunt 137 pounds! I had an upper respiratory infection until Thanksgiving. My school-aged kids, who were on their summer break from school, were continuously disappointed because Dad was not home to take them camping and fishing. All they recall was Dad coming home with a pack full of smokey-smelling clothes. By the next day Mom would have washed and dried his fire clothes so that he could repack his fire pack in preparation for the next fire dispatch. The next night the telephone would ring in the middle of the night. Dad would be absent from the breakfast table the next morning.

One day I spent the day with the Wise River timber assistant hiking cross-country into a proposed timber sale area. It was a long and tough hike. We returned to the ranger station at 5:30 p.m. that afternoon.

The district ranger ordered us to hike into a fire in the Anaconda Wilderness Area. He said our supper would be the C-rations in our fire packs. One portion of the eight-mile hike into the fire was a cross-country climb up a steep ridge. We arrived at the fire at 2:00 a.m. the following morning. We immediately assisted some smokejumpers already there dig fire line all night and throughout most of the morning. We finally ate our C-rations at noon.

On Labor Day weekend in 1967 I was a sector boss on the Trapper Creek Fire in Idaho. We had been helicoptered into the perimeter of the fire. Our assignment was to construct a containment line. On September first at 1:00 p.m., a strong wind hit the fire and it blew up. It rapidly grew to over 5,500 acres, traveling sixteen miles in nine hours! It even burned through the fire camp. The helicopter pilots flew out when they saw the fire approaching. We were marooned on the fire line with an injured firefighter. We had to spend the night there.

The next day we found many black rectangular marks in the fire camp bed grounds. They were the kapok sleeping bags that had burned up. Here and there were little piles of personal shaving and other gear at the head of the black rectangles that had been consumed by the fire.

The nearby Sundance Fire likewise blew up. It grew to over 56,000 acres. That fire overran a dozer operator and a sector boss, killing them both as they sought shelter under the dozer. Due to the blistered concrete deck and the fact that the fire cooked the temper out of the re-bar, it was estimated that the temperature around the Pack River Bridge reached around 2,000 degrees F.

Sundance Fire—Site of the two fatalities

Johnny Appleseed

I retired from the USDA Forest Service in May 1994. Because I held an air support group supervisor rating, a critical shortage category, I kept accepting fire assignments as a temporary State of Montana employee.

That summer I was dispatched to a fire on state land just south of Bonner, Montana. I was only on that fire for four days. Our camping area was located in a huge patch of spotted knapweed. Knapweed is an exotic invasive weed that is easily spread by humans and animals. In those days we firefighters received no instructions on how to prevent the spread of this weed.

Spotted knapweed.
PHOTO COURTESY BEAVERHEAD COUNTY

Shortly after I returned home, I was repacking my fire pack on my living room floor. I initially could not find my little Maglite flashlight. Then it hit me that it was probably in one of the inside pockets of the tent I carried to fires.

When I turned my tent inside out to look for my flashlight, knapweed seeds and stems poured onto my living room floor. I was stunned! In just four days my boots had dragged lots of potentially harmful knap weed seeds into my tent. GAWD! I had been accepting fire assignments from Florida to Alaska! Was I spreading this noxious weed across the continent?

I recently visited with a Forest Service hydrologist and a recently retired Bureau of Land Management employee. Both of them assured me that firefighters today are instructed on how to prevent the spread of noxious weeds. Mechanized equipment is steam cleaned before being dispatched to a fire. Things have changed for the better!

Artists

In the mid-nineties I was dispatched to a fire near Medford, Oregon. On the fire helibase was a southwest Indian helitack crew. Two of the Indians were exceptional artists. During slack times they would pencil gorgeous sketches of Native dancers. On completion of the sketches, the artists would wad up the sketches and throw them into the waste basket. When they left to fulfill a helicopter sling assignment, other helibase personnel would retrieve those discarded sketches.

Another assignment I had during this period was at a fire near Happy Camp, California, situated on the Klamath River. Dense afternoon smoke usually restricted helicopter flights to only four hours each morning. During slack times, some of us would sit on the riverbank and watch river otter hunt salmon.

Fire camp management had erected a triangular wooden structure made with three four-by-eight foot sheets of plywood which were covered with white butcher paper. Next to the plywood structure, a supply of colored felt-tip pens were available to anyone who wished to sketch something during slack time that followed dinner.

A National Guard unit was assigned to the fire. Among those in the unit was a talented artist who sketched some entertaining pictures. One was of a guardsman, with his back to the viewer, with burning trees in the background. A yellow stream went from the guardsman to the fire. The guardsman, looking over his shoulder, was saying, "Doing all we can to put out the fire." Another one of his sketches was a turtle making love to a guardsman helmet. The helmet resembled the shape of the turtle and covered in camouflage similar in color to the turtle. A stream of hearts rose from the turtle, and its little tail was wagging.

In 1996 I was assigned to a fire near Tofte, on the Superior National Forest in Minnesota. In the Plans Section was an artist whose duties included drawing a new picture for the cover of each day's shift plan. Examples of his work are depicted on the facing page. Sketches from June 1966 Incident Action Plans, South Temperance River Fire, Minnesota.

Credibility

From 1991 to1993, I was stationed as a forester on the Curlew Ranger District, which is part of the Colville National Forest, located north of Spokane, Washington.

One day I was assigned to scale (estimate the volume of logs) at the local sawmill. The logs had been harvested on national forest land. Scaling was part

Reference Point BY DENNIS

Night Watch BY DENNIS

of the process of determining the value of the harvested logs. I was standing in for the regular scaler who was on sick leave.

During the course of my estimating the volume of those logs for payment, I was approached by the sawmill owner. He pointed to a LARGE log with rot located in the center. He asked me what I estimated to be the net volume of the wood in that log. I suspected he was testing me. I asked him to write down what he thought was the net volume in that log.

I measured the log length, averaged the end diameters, looked up the gross volume on the log measurement scale stick, deducted the squared defect, and wrote down my estimate.

When I handed my answer to the mill owner, he exclaimed "That's close enough!" as he showed me the answer he'd already written down.

I grinned, knowing that I'd established my credibility with the sawmill owner.

Log Scale Measuring Stick. PHOTO COURTESY FORESTRY SUPPLIERS INC.

Coordination

In May 1988, I was dispatched to Duluth, Minnesota, to assist the Superior National Forest in their aviation program during an early fire season. At the time I was the forest aviation officer on the Beaverhead National Forest in Montana.

Early on I was asked to investigate an incident where Canadian aircraft get mixed in with our aircraft over the Grand Marias Ranger District. The fire was near the Canadian border and was threatening a logging camp in Canada. Because the retardant for the fire was being flown out of Duluth, I decided to drive out to the airport and visit with one of the air tanker pilots. At the airport, an air tanker pilot informed me that, during their retardant drop operations, Canadian water scooping aircraft and helicopters had entered the air space over the fire unannounced.

I then drove out to the Grand Marias district ranger office and visited with the district ranger. She filled me in on how the fire started, as well as on her request for a type II fire management team. She also informed about the team briefing and closeout.

The Canadians had as much or more resources on the fire than we had.

The Canadians had not been invited into the type II team briefing, nor were they invited to the team closeout where fire behavior, resources, and tactics were reviewed. Canadians even constructed an unapproved helicopter landing area in the Boundary Waters Canoe Wilderness Area!

The management of the fire was a shame on us, not a shame on the Canadians!

When I returned to Duluth, I found out a TFR (Temporary Flight Restriction) over the fire had not been filed with the FAA to prevent unauthorized aircraft from entering the airspace over the fire. I reviewed the Forest Aviation Plan, the Boundary Waters Canoe Wilderness Area Management Plan, and the Forest Safety Plan. None of them included a coordinating radio frequency for Canadian aircraft!

Before returning to Montana, at the request of the Superior National Forest, I wrote a letter recommending that various plans include a coordinating aircraft radio frequency for Canadians aircraft. I also recommended that, when Canadian resources enter the United States, a local resource advisor be assigned to them, and that a TFR be filed early for large fires.

I sent a copy of my letter to the Provincial Headquarters in Ottawa. The next year I ran into a Minnesota team on a fire near John Day, Oregon. They informed me that they learned from my letter.

Branding Ax

During the 1980s I was employed as a forester on the Beaverhead National Forest in Montana. One day I was attempting to locate a section corner east of Winkley Camp, located in Gorge Creek, in the East Pioneer Mountains. Winkley Camp had been the location of a sawmill.

In the course of my search, I discovered a lodgepole pine tree that had been marked for cutting but left untouched.

I suspect the tree was bypassed in favor of harvesting the larger spruce trees. The lodgepole had been marked for cutting by stamping it with a U.S. brand using a branding ax.

The brand was stamped on an ax blaze. This was a common method of designating trees for cutting prior to the use of tree marking paint. A brand

Above: Branding ax poll (head)

Right: Stamped U.S. brand on lower right

would also be applied below stump height, which would serve as proof that the harvested tree had been designated for cutting.

Four Strand

In the fall of 1963 I was transferred from the Colville National Forest (north of Spokane) to the Madison Ranger District, headquartered in Ennis, Montana. The Madison District was part of the Beaverhead National Forest (now the Beaverhead-Deerlodge National Forest) in southwest Montana.

My task was to prepare and administer timber sales.

At that time a mountain pine beetle infestation was reaching epidemic proportions in the vast stands of lodgepole pines in the Island Park Ranger District (part of the Targhee National Forest in Idaho). The Island Park Ranger District is south of and adjacent to the Madison Ranger District.

Our forest timber staff person was concerned about the beetle epidemic and so he arranged for me to visit the Targhee Ranger District to see how the district was responding to the beetle epidemic, and also how they were dealing with dwarf mistletoe. Dwarf mistletoe infects and sometimes stunts the growth of and/or kills lodgepole pine. It was widely speculated that it was just a matter of time before the beetle epidemic in Idaho would spread northward into Montana and then to the Beaverhead National Forest.

A group of us, which included the Targhee National Forest timber staff person and the Island Park District ranger, were standing on the edge of a forest road discussing the situation. The Island Park District was laying out HUGE clear cuts (some as large as 1,000 acres) on their flat terrain in order to slow down the spread of the beetle and mistletoe infestations.

Mountain Pine Beetle (.2 inch).
PHOTO COURTESY D. KUCHARSKI K. KUCHARSKA/SHUTTERSTOCK.

Dwarf mistletoe.
PHOTO COURTESY CHRISTOPHER FOELKER, USDA FOREST SERVICE

As we looked over the dying forest that spread out below us, I noticed a brand new four-strand barbed wire fence threading its way through the beetle-infested, red-needled, and dying lodgepole pine tree stand.

I explained to the group that this new fence would end up smashed down to the ground in ten years as the dying trees fell on top of it! The Targhee Forest personnel, new to the beetle epidemic, were shocked! They never considered the threat to the barbed wire fences they were building within the dying timber stands. I suggested they take lessons from the folks in the Big Hole Valley in southwest Montana. The Big Hole Valley had been host to this type of massive beetle epidemic in the 1930s. Fences constructed in the timber since then were strong log fences able to withstand most falling trees.

Response

In the 1980s, I was employed by the Beaverhead National Forest in Dillon, Montana. One of my duties was to coordinate motorized travel restrictions among nine agencies that manage lands or roads in the vicinity of the Beaverhead National Forest.

These agencies include the USDA's Forest Service and its Agricultural Research Service; the Department of Interior's Bureau of Land Management, its National Park Service, and its Bureau of Reclamation; the U.S. Fish & Wildlife Service's National Wildlife Refuge System; the Montana Department of Fish, Wildlife, and Parks; the Montana Department of Natural Resource & Conservation; and Beaverhead County.

One example of a problem that can occur due to lack of coordination is illustrated by what occurred during the 1980s on Fleecer Mountain (about seventeen miles southwest of Butte, Montana). Motorized access to public lands located on the upper elevations of the mountain was delayed by two weeks until the public lands parcels located at the lower elevations of the mountain became open.

One of my satisfying endeavors was convincing district rangers to support a proposal (which proved to be a contentious one) to prohibit gasoline powered motorboats on small lakes located on national forest land. An example of the negative impacts that these motorboats were having on these small lakes was evident on Lower Miner Lake, west of Jackson, Montana. The lake's surface was littered with fragmented vegetation chopped up by motorboat propellers. Patches of engine exhaust oil were also visible on the surface of the lake. Aquatic loving animals and birds were sparse, apparently avoiding the motorboat traffic. The otherwise quiet atmosphere in the adjacent campground was disrupted by early morning and evening motorboat traffic. The lake shore was beaten bare of vegetation and some shorelines were eroding from the slapping of waves caused by motorboat wakes.

Within one year following the enforcement of the gasoline motorboat prohibition on Miner Lake (electric motors could still be used), the environmental response was amazing! Beavers moved in and constructed a huge lodge in the outlet. A river otter took up residence in an abandoned beaver lodge near the lake inlet. (One day it led me in my canoe away from the lodge, and then it returned to the lodge. Could there have been young ones in the lodge?)

One gorgeous day I paddled my canoe up to a gentleman sitting in an inflated inner tube in the middle of the lake. I asked him what he thought of the motorboat restrictions. He said it was the best decision the Forest Service had ever made!

The Skunk Fire

In the early 1980s a ranch hand chased a skunk into a culvert located on the ranch. The ranch is located about twelve miles north of Wisdom, Montana.

The ranch hand was so intent on killing that skunk that he threw gasoline into the culvert entrance. After the ranch hand lit the gasoline, flames blew out the far end of the culvert and ignited the grass in the hay meadow!

Pushed by a strong prevailing southwest wind, the flames raced across the hay meadow and spread onto the adjacent national forest land!

The fire grew so large that several hundred men, along with a fire management team, were called in to fight the fire.

I was later informed that the company that insured the ranch ended up reimbursing the U.S. Government $350,000 for having fought that fire.

Chapter Seven

ASSISTING GAME WARDENS & BIG GAME BIOLOGISTS

FOLLOWING MY RETIREMENT from the USDA Forest Service in 1994, I was assisting Montana Fish Wildlife & Parks game wardens and big game biologists.

Public Access

In the early 1990s I was invited to give a presentation on map and compass to the annual Region 3 Montana game wardens' summer meeting at the Wall Creek Wildlife Management Area. Chad Murphy was one of the attendees at the meeting. Chad was a Montana Fish, Wildlife & Parks investigator stationed at Whitehall, Montana.

That fall I received a request from Chad to assist him in determining land ownership in the Boulder Valley, where he had been confronted by a local rancher who had accused him of trespassing. The rancher apparently had a strong prejudice against anyone who worked for a public agency, including game wardens and Forest Service employees. Chad, who was new to the area, told the rancher he was checking on bow hunters on what he thought was state land. The rancher told Chad "You really don't know where you are, do you, son?" Chad said he wasn't sure, but he would find out!

I agreed to meet Chad the next day at the Whitehall truck stop.

After meeting Chad at the truck stop, we proceeded to the local Forest Service office where I obtained a USGS topographic map that covered Chad's area of concern. We drove to the area where Chad had been confronted. The tops of the fence posts on either side of the gate which provided entry into the area were painted orange, which is how a private landowner in Montana can signal a "No Trespassing" warning. This is regarded to be a private landowner's legal way to show that the area behind the orange fence posts is private land and closed to public entry.

We drove into the area and stopped where Chad had been challenged. Using the coordinates from my GPS receiver, I plotted our location on the topographic map. I informed Chad that the point where we were standing was one hundred yards inside of the state lands boundary line. We were not trespassing on private land! Chad thanked me and said he would follow up.

Chad later informed me that the rancher did indeed have a permit to graze on that portion of state land. However, the rancher did not have the authority to mark that area as if it were his own private land, nor was he allowed to mark the area in a manner that would falsely prohibit public entry through that gate. The state fined the rancher $100 for violating the terms of his grazing permit and put him on probation. He was also ordered to remove or paint over the orange paint on the gate posts.

Male Scar

One weekend I was helping out at a game station in the Ruby Valley, located about fifteen miles south of Alder, Montana. A suburban truck pulled up with Butte license plates. In the truck were four men, including a teenage hunter who had suffered a rifle telescopic scope cut above one eye.

I advised the hunter with the scope cut to be proud of the injury, as it would heal up to be the second most common male scar in Montana.

Gone!

One weekend I was assisting MFWP Big Game Biologist Bob Brannon at a check station in the Ruby Valley. Around mid-afternoon a hunter in a pickup with Montana license plates approached our check station. In the bed of the pickup were two cow elk. I asked the driver, who was from Whitehall, Montana, and had properly tagged his elk, "Who did the second elk belong to?"

The driver explained that a pair of out-of-state hunters had informed him that they did not have room to transport their cow elk in their camp trailer and asked him if he would transport their elk to Whitehall, where they had been staying at a motel. He also stated that they should not be too far behind him, as they were also on their way out. I asked the hunter from Whitehall to stay put until we had an opportunity to interview those two out-of-state hunters.

Shortly thereafter, a pickup truck pulling a camp trailer approached our check station. Two large men got out of the truck and approached me while Bob was busy interviewing other hunters.

The two hunters, who smelled strongly of liquor, stated they were Alaskan fishermen. I inquired which one of them had shot and tagged the second elk that was being transported in the Whitehall man's pickup. One of the hunters stated it was his. I then asked the hunter if he had shot that cow elk in the Ruby River drainage. He replied, "Yes." I then asked the hunter if he had a cow permit for that elk. The hunter blurted out, "My hunting permit says ELK, and BY GAWD that's what I shot!" I calmly explained to him that in the Ruby-Red Rock Hunting District hunters are required to have a special cow permit to harvest a cow elk.

I then called Bob over to handle what was becoming a tense situation. After a short, heated discussion, Bob informed the hunter he would have to seize the elk as evidence. Then Bob asked me to load that seized elk into his MFWP pickup truck while he interviewed some approaching hunters. I turned to the Alaskan hunters and asked them if they would assist me in loading the seized elk into Bob's truck. They rudely denied my request. (Expletive deleted.)

I took the Whitehall hunter aside and quietly explained to him that he could be cited for transporting an illegally harvested elk. HOWEVER, if he would be willing to help me load the elk into Bob's truck, we would be willing to overlook his violation. The hunter was all too willing to cooperate with me, and he hastily helped me transfer that elk from his truck into Bob's truck.

Then he was GONE!

Priorities

In 1997, on the Saturday following Thanksgiving, I was working at a check station south of the Ruby River Reservoir. Late in the morning several hunters, who were headed home, stopped at the check station. They had been camped near the Forest Service Divide rental cabin (which is on the Madison Ranger District) while they were hunting the upper Ruby River drainage. They informed me that the Divide Cabin had burned down on Thanksgiving Eve and that they had assisted the couple who had been run out of the cabin by the fire. Mark Petroni, who was the Madison District ranger at the time, provided me with the details.

A couple from Ennis, Montana, had rented the cabin in order to hunt in the area. On Thanksgiving Eve, as they were preparing to go to bed, a wood fire was burning in the cabin heating stove. They had placed a five-gallon propane bottle in the cabin's open sleeping loft and connected a rubber propane line to a lantern suspended above the wood stove. They could smell propane gas, so the husband shook the hose, which immediately became disconnected. Not only was there a rush of propane, but the lantern was extinguished as well. The escaping gas began to fill the room. Fumbling in the dark, the husband grabbed his rifle, his expensive Swarovski spotting scope, and his wife (speculation has it was probably in that order), and they both charged out of the cabin. The cabin was immediately consumed in fire, leaving the couple standing in the snow in stocking feet and underwear.

Fortunately, the hunters that were camped nearby ran over to assist the couple. The couple's pickup was close to the cabin and in danger of igniting from the radiant heat. One of the hunters asked the husband where the truck ignition keys were located. The husband pointed to the burning cabin and said they were in the cabin inside his pants pocket! They broke one of the truck's windows in order to put the transmission in neutral so they could push it to safety.

The cabin was a total loss. The following summer a loader was borrowed from the nearby Red Rocks Lake National Wildlife Refuge in order to excavate the ruins. A cinder block foundation was constructed and lodgepole pine logs were obtained for the new cabin. The new cabin was built by volunteers at Vigilante Station, located about ten miles north of the Divide Cabin site. The manufactured logs were moved to Divide in 1999. Construction was completed in 2001.

After this episode, the district started providing small propane cylinders and asked renters not to bring their own propane. This was later followed by the Beaverhead-Deerlodge National Forest requiring cabin renters to provide small propane cylinders for the cook stove and gas lights.

Divide Cabin replacement under construction.
PHOTO COURTESY U.S. FOREST SERVICE

Completed Divide Cabin replacement. PHOTO COURTESY U.S. FOREST SERVICE

Warden Kerry Wahl portaging my canoe up from Hidden Lake

Mason jar camp coffee maker

Chapter Eight

HUNTING & FISHING

The Magpie

I ATTENDED MONTANA STATE UNIVERSITY (now called the University of Montana—Missoula) in the late 1950s. One of our classmates, Tom Uphill, was a Canadian from Fernie, British Columbia. His father owned a hunter and guiding outfitting business in Fernie.

Some students who hunted would obtain their wild meat in the fall, then move off campus, rent an apartment, and live off the wild meat for the balance of the school year.

We would invite Tom to accompany us on elk hunts. Tom could not hunt because he was not a Montana resident. He was happy to accompany us for the camaraderie and the outdoor experience. We were pleased to have Tom along because he would help us pack out our elk. We would share some of our meat with him. Besides, having been raised by a hunting and outfitting family, Tom was an exceptional outdoorsman, and would quietly share his outdoor skills with us.

Tom would salvage the liver, heart, kidneys, and tongue from our kills. We nicknamed Tom "The Magpie," comparing him to the bird species that cleans the carcasses of all remaining morsels from gut piles hunters leave behind.

All of us would use pack frames to pack out our elk quarters. Tom had a unique way of packing out the first elk quarter. He would establish shoulder straps by cutting slits in the hide. He knew just how to position the shoulder straps so as to balance the load. The elk hide provided Tom with a sack in which to pack out the elk quarter. A rough sketch of the method is to the right.

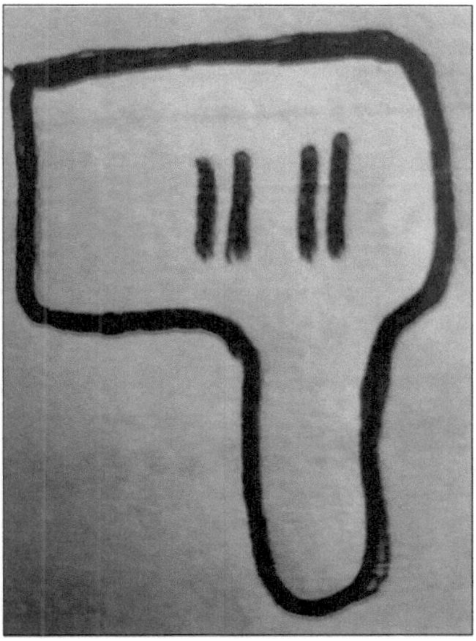

Personal sketch

Almond Joy

In the 1990s my wife Pat and I decided to go elk hunting in the head of Scudder Creek. Scudder Creek is in the Grasshopper Valley, about twenty miles southwest of Dillon, Montana. We parked my Bronco truck in the West Fork of Dyce Creek, next to the old tungsten mine.

We then hiked west over a ridge, near the Beaverhead National Forest boundary, and dropped into a long stringer meadow in the head of Scudder Creek. It was a gorgeous day with fresh snow on the ground.

After hunting for several hours, we broke for lunch, sitting in the sun below the timber on the southwest slope of Scudder Creek. After lunch I decided to take a little nap in the sunshine.

I was dozing off when Pat nudged me and asked, "Did you hear that?" I responded, "Hear what?" Then I heard a child's voice shouting "Dad!" Joking, I told Pat it must be a bird's call and pretended to resume my snooze. Pat shoved me and demanded that I walk out into the meadow and call the child down to the meadow.

Upon entering the meadow, I heard the child call "Dad!' again, followed by a rifle shot. I shouted for the child to walk downhill to me.

A woman, carrying a rifle and leading a five-year-old boy, emerged from the timber. They were both dressed well. I asked the woman where they were from and how they became lost. The woman explained that she and her husband owned a saloon in Scobey, Montana. She and her husband and son were guests at a ranch in the Grasshopper Valley. She could not recall the name of the ranch. She said the ranch house was an old log home. I replied, "Hah! The Zimdar Ranch!" She explained that her husband drove her and her son to the top of the ridge above Scudder Creek. Upon parking the truck, he instructed her and her son to hunt in one direction, and he would hunt in the other direction. She was unfamiliar with the area and had no map or compass!

I offered to take the woman and her son to our Bronco parked in Dyce Creek and drive them around to the Zimdar Ranch. I gave her son an Almond Joy in order to cheer him up. I then offered to carry the woman's rifle. As a safety precaution, I ejected the chambered cartridge and removed the magazine.

Upon arriving at the Zimdar Ranch, I immediately called the sheriff's office and suggested that, if they got a call from a husband reporting his wife and son were lost, to inform him they were back at the Zimdar Ranch. As I was leaving the ranch, the woman thanked me. I told her she owed me a beer.

About ten years later a student from Scobey was enrolled in my college Map, Compass & GPS class. I told him the story of the lost mother and son and informed him he was welcome to walk into the woman's saloon and collect my beer. He told me that he knew the woman. She had since divorced her husband, but still owned the saloon.

Gut Piles

Some years ago, Frank Fowler and I left town early in his truck to go elk hunting. The weather conditions were perfect. About six inches of snow had fallen during the night. The temperature was in the teens, and there was only a slight wind.

As we were driving up the Reservoir Creek Road west of Bannack, Montana, a hunter was following close behind us, his bright lights reflecting off our rearview mirrors. (He just HAD to get there first!)

I suggested to Frank that he pull over and let the impatient hunter go by us. Frank pulled over, and the hunter roared by us, snow swirling in his taillights.

It wasn't too long after we parked at the head of Watson Creek that about four elk came charging up the slope about fifty yards south of us. Both Frank and I stepped off the road and each of us dropped a cow elk.

Two elk in the back of Frank's truck. PHOTO COURTESY FRANK FOWLER

At Frank's suggestion, we dragged the elk over to the road and gutted the elk out next to the road. We hoped that the impatient hunter would see the steaming gut piles on his way out.

Long Shot

About thirty years ago, I decided to go elk hunting in Riley Canyon. Riley Canyon is located in the Blacktail Mountains, twelve miles southeast of Dillon, Montana. My plan was to arrive at daybreak in a saddle on the south side of the drainage. My hope was to intercept elk being chased up from the flats below.

It had snowed about six inches the night before. I had to chain up the rear tires on my Ford Bronco in order to reach the edge of the timber. I could see that there were fresh tire tracks ahead of me. Chaining up put me about ten minutes behind.

There was a pickup truck parked at the edge of the timber when I arrived there. I followed the hunter's tracks. It appeared the hunter was headed for the same saddle!

About ten minutes before I was planning to arrive at the saddle, daylight was starting to break, and I heard a rifle shot coming from the saddle. Dang! When I arrived at the saddle, I could see where the hunter had sat down in the snow to make his LONG shot south across a small drainage. The hunter was approaching an elk he had downed on the other side of the drainage.

Intending to help the hunter dress out his elk, I followed his tracks around the head of the drainage and approached the hunter from above. The hunter was bent over, tagging his elk. His rifle was resting on an extended bi-pod. He never heard me approach him. I quietly placed my pack in the snow, opened it up, and pulled out a thermos of hot chocolate. After pouring a cup of hot chocolate, I said, "Congratulations!" Startled, the hunter turned around to see me grinning and extending him a cup of hot chocolate.

I helped the hunter dress out his elk. The hunter was a bartender from Butte. He had shot the elk from a distance of about 700 yards with his .264 Winchester Magnum.

The hunter informed me he returned each year to hunt elk from that same saddle. He knew the distance to where he would most likely intercept an elk. He sighted in his rifle prior to hunting season on a discarded and tipped-over used refrigerator positioned at that distance.

The hunter would return the next day with a horse to skid the elk down to the flats below the elk.

Poncho's Goat

In October of 2022, as I was leaving the Den Restaurant in Dillon, Montana, I met Poncho and Bev McCoy at the door. I hadn't seen these dear friends for over twenty years. They were currently living in Oregon. In the course of a quick conversation, Bev informed me that their daughter was married to a former smokejumper.

I quickly returned to the restaurant to gift a book to the McCoys. I had written the book titled *Smokejumper & Other Stories.*

While I was signing the book, Poncho reminded me that I had directed him into a mountain goat.

In 1996, I met Poncho checking out of a ranch supply store. He informed me that he had a goat permit for the East Pioneer Mountains, west of Melrose,

Montana. I informed Poncho that when he finished checking out of the store I would meet him at the local sporting goods store, where he would purchase a USGS topographic map, and I would place an X on the map where he could shoot a goat.

At the sporting goods store, Poncho purchased a copy of the Mount Tahepia topographic map. On the map I placed an X on the south slope of Sharp Mountain. I informed Poncho that I had seen mountain goats in that area from a Forest Service aircraft while on a fire detection patrol. I also informed him he could unload his horses at the Mono Creek campground, then ride up the Jacobsen Creek trail to Tahepia Lake, where he could set up camp and picket his horses. Tahepia Lake is only a mile south of Sharp Mountain.

About a week after the opening of the goat hunting season, Poncho called me to inform me he had shot a mountain goat on my X with his bow! The goat broke off a portion of one horn when it fell. However, there was enough length on the intact horn that the goat made it into the *Pope & Young* record book!

Poncho's Goat. PHOTO COURTESY PONCHO MCCOY

Honey Hole

On the south end of the Gravelly Mountain Range on the Beaverhead-Deerlodge National Forest is a chain of seven lakes. These lakes are about forty miles south of Ennis, Montana, and are comprised of Elk, Hidden, Goose, Otter, Cliff, Wade, and Smith Lakes.

Jim

On numerous occasions, approaching from the Centennial Valley, I would drive to the end of the road just south of Hidden Lake to portage my fourteen-foot Winona kevlar canoe (thirty-four pounds) one quarter-mile down to Hidden Lake. I would then paddle to the north end of the lake and portage my canoe about one mile to Goose and Otter Lakes and fish those lakes.

In August 1998, I took Beaverhead National Forest Fisheries Biologist Jim Brammer and Henry Hoffman into Otter Lake to show them a unique phenomenon. Near the north end of the lake is a deep hole about fifteen feet in diameter. I called it a "honey hole." The rest of the lake is only about three feet deep. Rainbow trout would venture out of the hole to feed in the shallow parts of the lake. If they felt threatened by an osprey or other predator, they would dash back into the hole. If the threat persisted, they would nervously swim around in the hole. This would stir up the silt, making it difficult for a predator to see down into the hole!

Jim was AMAZED! He had never seen such a phenomenon! I explained to Jim that I would paddle up to the edge of the hole and drop a hook baited with worms into the hole. The limit of five fish was caught in about twenty minutes!

On the way home Jim informed me that he was going to request that Montana Fish, Wildlife & Parks establish a one-fish limit on the lake. He did not want me cleaning out the honey hole!

Dang! He got it done! The current limit on Otter Lake is "1 rainbow trout daily and in possession" (2023 FWP Montana Fishing Regulations, p. 67).

Henry

Awyhee Lake

In August 1995, my friend Ron Primozic invited me to accompany him on a four-day canoe and fishing trip on Lake Owyhee, which is located in southeast Oregon.

Chukar. PHOTO COURTESY LUC COEKAERTS

Lake Owyhee is fifty-three miles long and famous for its largemouth bass fishing. It is also noted for its abundance of Chukar game birds and rattlesnakes. Golden eagles, wild horses, coyotes, mountain lions, pronghorn antelope, mule deer, ground squirrels, rabbits, and California big horn sheep also inhabit the area.

We camped near the upper (south end) of the lake near a privately-owned cabin. The nearby outhouse had no door (a room with a view). To maximize our exploring opportunities, Ron's canoe had a 4 HP Johnson outboard motor mounted on it.

Both of us being licensed pilots, the highlight of our trip was discovering a dirt aircraft runway and a nearby deserted cabin. Both the cabin and the runway are located close to the lake shore.

In the cabin we found a visitors' logbook. A hilarious entry was made by a pilot who related how he met a woman in a bar in Ontario, Oregon. One thing led to another, and in the course of pitching some woo, he talked the woman into flying into Lake Owyhee in his Cessna 180. They spent a cozy night together in that deserted cabin!

The area was spectacular and wild. The only fish we caught were two suckers!

In spite of our poor fishing success, we enjoyed exploring this wild and gorgeous area.

Lake Owyhee, canoe, cabin & outhouse with a view

Cutthroat

In 1992 the Bureau of Land Management (BLM) in southwestern Montana acquired 400 acres, which they added to an area now totaling about 7,800 acres called Axolotl Lakes. This area is located about ten miles southwest of Ennis, Montana, and is classified by the BLM as a Wilderness Study Area (WSA).

The area includes a beautiful cabin. In about 2004 the BLM turned the cabin into a rental cabin for public use. The cabin overlooks Twin Lakes. Reservoir Lake is also located in the area. Three additional lakes (Grassy, Axolotl, and Blue Lake) are also within the WSA. Motorized access is permitted on the way to the cabin and on a few other limited routes. The rest of the area is walk-in only.

In September 2003, my friend Ron Primozic and I hiked about two miles into Axolotl Lake. After lunch, Ron prepared to go fishing. I decided to take a nap.

I'd no sooner dozed off when I was awakened to Ron shouting he had a big one on his line (which he'd hooked on his third cast). He had hooked a huge Yellowstone cutthroat!

We took the fish to the nearby fish hatchery to get it weighed and measured. It weighed nine-and-one-quarter pounds, was twenty-four inches in length, and sixteen-and-one-quarter inches in girth.

Ron Primozic with Yellowstone cutthroat

First Elk

In the early part of the 1970s, I was a forester for the USDA Forest Service stationed on the Beaverhead National Forest. My office was at the forest supervisor's office in Dillon, Montana.

One Friday, at the end of the workday, I had just returned to my office. Ray Behnert, the forest landscape architect, was about to leave the office. I asked Ray if he had ever shot an elk. He replied, "No, I never have." I explained to him that I had been checking on road construction into a timber sale in Mule Creek. (Mule Creek flows into Birch Creek, in the East Pioneer Mountains, which is located about twenty miles northwest of Dillon.) I informed Ray that I had noticed a lot of fresh elk sign at the head of Mule Creek. I went on to tell Ray that the general hunting season opened up that coming Sunday. I invited him to accompany me on a hunt. He gladly accepted the invitation!

Sunday morning, at O-dark thirty, we departed Dillon in my Ford Bronco. After parking my Bronco at the end of a newly constructed road at daybreak, we proceeded to follow elk tracks in the new fresh snow. Hunting conditions were perfect!

We had walked only about ten minutes when a five-point bull elk jumped up out of its bed. Ray got off the first shot and downed the elk. He was absolutely elated, and amazed at the size of the animal he had just put down. I educated him on how to dress out and quarter an elk.

After quartering up the elk, we returned to my Bronco to retrieve my plastic sled so we could more easily slide the quarters to my Bronco.

We loaded the elk quarters into the top carrier of my Bronco and we were back in Dillon by noon!

Ray gave me half the elk. Boy, did he have an elk story to tell!

Round-A-Pound

My first year of hunting in Montana was in 1958 when I was a forestry student at Montana State University (now called The University of Montana—Missoula).

Some of us students would hunt big game, and if successful, move out of the dorms and finish the academic year in a rental, living on wild game and potatoes.

That first year I hunted with a .30-30 Winchester, expending thirty-five rounds that hunting season in order to finally bag my first elk. The word got around campus about the number of rounds it took me to get my elk. I was referred to as "Round-a-Pound Swede."

In 1993 another fellow and I were hunting elk in the Grasshopper Valley, about twenty-four miles west of Dillon, Montana. I was hunting below a patch of timber, and my hunting partner was in the timber above me. He jumped a bunch of elk. I heard him empty the magazine on his Winchester Model 88. A cow elk tore out of the timber in front of me, which I downed with my .338-06. After downing the cow elk, I watched a wounded spike bull elk run out of the timber, run downhill close to me, and cross a draw below me. A hunter from Ohio finished off the wounded bull as it ran up the slope on the other side of the draw.

My hunting partner walked down to me as I was dressing out my elk. He inquired as to why I didn't finish off the wounded bull. I replied that first of all, I didn't know, given all of his shooting, if hadn't already killed another elk up there in the timber. Secondly, I'd already killed my own elk and it would have been against hunting regulations for me to kill a second elk to help another hunter fill his tag.

Given all the rounds my partner expended, I informed him he qualified to be called "Round-a-Pound."

Chapter Nine

RESCUE

Red Asphalt

IN THE MID-EIGHTIES, late one afternoon, two of us volunteers on the local ambulance responded to a motorcycle wreck located on Interstate 15, just north of the High Bridge. The High Bridge crosses the Beaverhead River, about one mile north of Clark Canyon Reservoir, in Beaverhead County, Montana.

Motorcycle wrecks are usually messy, so we expected to find the worst.

On approaching the accident scene, we could see traffic was stopped, and vehicle lights were flashing. As we crept into the accident scene, we viewed a long streak of blood on the asphalt. The thought crossed my mind, "Gawd, what do we have here?"

As we parked the ambulance, the motorcycle driver climbed out of the ditch beside the highway. He was wearing a helmet with a chin guard and dressed in a leather suit. He was covered with deer entrails and blood. He explained to us that he was traveling about 70 mph when a deer jumped over his motorcycle. His rearview mirror sliced open the deer's abdomen, and its entrails and blood dumped on him.

The driver was shook, but other than a few scrapes, he was fine. His protective gear saved him from serious injury or death. We were relieved to return to Dillon without a patient.

Why Me?

In the 1980s, as a volunteer EMT on the local ambulance in Dillon, Montana, I was dispatched to the Metlen Hotel to pick up a patient who had collapsed in the hotel lobby.

Metlen Hotel

When I arrived at the hotel, I observed a gentleman lying unconscious on the lobby floor. A woman, who appeared to be of Native American descent, was laying her hands on the patient and mumbling that the man was her uncle.

After my attendant and I loaded the patient on the ambulance cot, I turned to the woman and asked her if she wanted to accompany us to the hospital. She accepted the offer and got in the front seat with me.

Upon arriving at the hospital, we wheeled the patient into the emergency room (ER). The woman wanted to accompany the patient into the ER but was told by the no-nonsense nurse to wait out in the hall.

After stabilizing the patient, the nurse and I wheeled him into the elevator to transport him into a room on the second floor. The woman accompanied us in the elevator.

As we were wheeling the patient into a room on the second floor, the woman tried to follow him into the room. The nurse, by now thoroughly exasperated with this woman, refused to let her in the room. The woman said, "At least give me his boots." The nurse turned to me and said, "Swede, please get this woman out of here." I turned to the woman and offered to give her a ride back to the ambulance garage downtown. She accepted the offer and got into the ambulance front seat, sliding up AGAINST me and putting a hand on my lap.

As we traveled back to the garage, the woman told me she was staying at the Metlen Hotel, and she suggested I come visit her. She also mentioned that she had just been released from a hospital. When I inquired as to whether she had been in a vehicle accident, she replied, "No, in a knife fight." I thought to myself, "God, why me?"

As we traveled downtown I saw a police car pass by me headed towards the hospital. (The nurse had earlier called the police about this woman.) I picked up the radio mike and said, "18-10, follow me back to the garage." In the rear view mirror I watched the patrol car execute a U-turn and begin to follow us to the garage. The woman asked, "What's going on, honey?" I replied, "I was just saying hello to the police."

When we arrived at the garage, I jumped out of the ambulance and told the policemen, "Take her!"

I found out the woman had served time in prison and was on probation. She was in possession of the patient's wallet and ring. I suspect she wanted the patient's boots so she could hock them at Gracie's secondhand store. The patient was not her uncle.

Dale Zink

Some folks who view my LA Rams team ball cap ask me if I am a Rams fan. "No," I reply, "I got this cap at a funeral."

In 2019 I attended a funeral in Dillon, Montana, for Dale Zink. Dale was a Rams fan, and the family had Rams caps for EVERYONE at the funeral! Dale had been a local high school counselor prior to his retirement. For many summers Dale worked for the Beaverhead National Forest as a dispatcher and aerial observer, patrolling and looking for forest fires.

Dale was dispatching on Saturday, August 9th, 1975, when I helped organize the rescue of country western singer Hank Williams, Jr. At the time I was a Beaverhead National Forest Service employee who volunteered in local search and rescue, as an EMT on our local ambulance, and as a ski patrolman.

Dale called me at home around 3:00 p.m. and informed me that Hank had fallen and seriously injured himself above Ajax Lake, west of Jackson, Montana. Hal Wetzsteon, the Wisdom Ranger District fire control officer, called Dale requesting that we organize a rescue operation.

Dale informed me that our patrol plane, a Cessna 182, was waiting for me at the Dillon airport to fly me to Wisdom. He informed me there were only six hours of daylight flying light left for our permitted flying! I grabbed some basic rescue equipment and raced out to the airport. We departed the airport at 3:30 p.m. While flying to Wisdom, Dale and I worked out the details of the rescue plan. Dale informed me he had ordered a Bell 47 helicopter (similar to one used in Korea) from Hamilton, Montana, to meet me at the Wisdom airport.

Basic backcountry rescue equipment used to rescue Hank (scoop stretcher, sleeping bag, poly pad, and jump kit)

In the course of the successful rescue Dale had wisely ordered three different aircraft (our Cessna 182, the Bell 47 helicopter, and a Bell 205 Huey helicopter). After transporting

Hank Williams, Jr., rescue, August 9, 1975. PHOTO COURTESY FRED BRIDENSTINE

Hank from Ajax Lake to Wisdom in the Bell 47 helicopter, we loaded Hank into the Cessna and flew to the Missoula airport. After landing at the airport, we taxied to the smokejumper base. Thanks to Dale, a Huey helicopter was warmed up and waiting for us to transport Hank and me to the Community Hospital in Missoula.

After leaving Hank at the hospital, I was helicoptered back to the smokejumper base. Upon boarding the Cessna, I was returned to Dillon with thirty minutes of flying light remaining!

Dale did such a great job of dispatching, I wrote him a Letter of Commendation.

At Dale's funeral I read the Letter of Commendation to the family. I also made a copy of the dispatch log Dale kept during the rescue of Hank. I gave them both to his daughter, whereupon she gave me a big hug!

HANK WILLIAMS JR. RESCUE
AUGUST 9, 1975

Aircraft Type	Mileage & Time Logs Nautical[1] /Statute/Minutes
Dillon to Wisdom (Fixed Wing—Cessna 182)	39/45/20
Wisdom to Ajax Lake & Return (Bell 47G-3B Helicopter)	31/36/30
Wisdom to Missoula (Fixed Wing—Cessna 182)	83/95/45
Community Hospital (Bell 205 Helicopter)	02/02/05

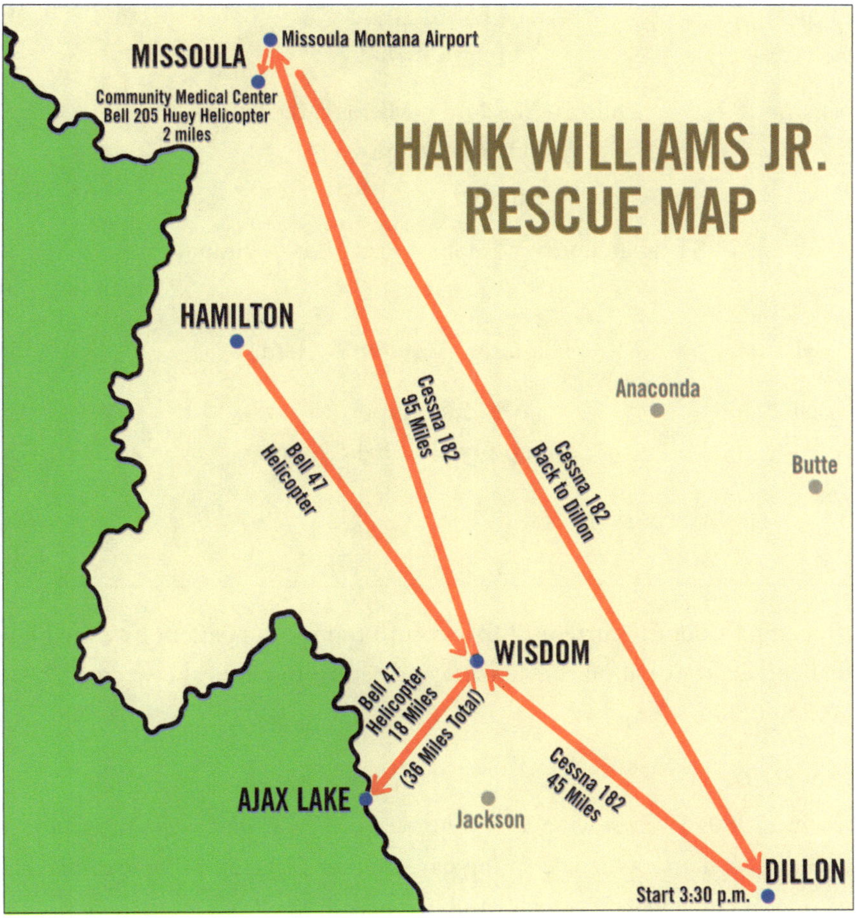

[1] One Nautical Mile = 1.15 Statute Miles

Comparison

What follows is in response to a local inquiry as to what the aircraft costs were in order to rescue Hank Williams, Jr., in 1975.

The aircraft and the fuel truck costs billed to Hank are derived from the 1975 aircraft flight invoices.

HANK WILLIAMS, JR RESCUE, 8/9/1975
AIRCRAFT RESCUE COSTS

Type	**Destinations** (Montana)	**Time** Minutes	**Cost** $
Cessna 182	Dillon—Wisdom—Missoula & Return (Depart Dillon 1523, Return 2041 = 5 hrs 18 min.	139	187
[2]Bell 47 G3 B1	Hamilton—Wisdom—Ajax Lake—Wisdom & Return	180	550
Fuel Truck	Hamilton–Wisdom & Return		38
[2]Bell 205	Missoula Airport to Community Hospital & Return	12	65
			Total 840

In comparison, the current (2024) cost to transport a patient by a life flight helicopter from Dillon to Missoula and return to base is between $50,000 and $60,000.

Scours

In the 1980s I was serving as a volunteer EMT on our local ambulance in Dillon, Montana. One late spring day, another EMT and I were dispatched to a local ranch where a ranch hand had been injured.

[2] Helicopter

It had been raining several days prior to the accident. A pair of ranch hands had been sorting yearlings and calves in a corral. Many of the calves were suffering from scours, causing them to defecate loose poop that was a mixture of stinky green, yellow, and brown. The cattle had been milling around all morning in the muddy corral, which had become a deep soup of mud thoroughly mixed with excrement.

The ranch hands had moved the yearlings into an adjoining corral. When one ranch hand was closing the corral gate, something spooked the yearlings. The yearlings panicked and pressed hard against the gate, breaking the gate latch and causing the gate to snap open, hitting the ranch hand in the face and tossing him into the mud.

As we approached the corral, the uninjured ranch hand started to pick up his injured partner. Seeing what appeared to be a broken nose I shouted to the ranch hand not to move his injured partner. My concern was that the injured man might have fractured his cervical spine, which could potentially be a very serious injury.

Using a scoop stretcher, we carefully scooped up the patient, taking care to immobilize his head and neck. As we scooped up the patient, some smelly brown, yellow, and green mud was also scooped up.

We transported him to the hospital emergency room. When we split the scoop stretcher to release the patient onto examining table, a large wad of stinky, colored mud also fell onto the examining table. Nurses turned their heads and closed their eyes, wincing as they removed the patient's stinky mud-caked boots and coveralls.

A nurse later quipped to me we should have run the patient through a car wash before we brought him in!

Subsequent examination of the patient revealed that he did indeed have a fracture of his cervical spine. Because he was a veteran, he was transferred to the Fort Harrison Hospital in Helena for treatment of his broken neck.

Oh, By the Way

In early 1990 I served as a volunteer EMT on the local ambulance in Dillon, Montana. One Sunday morning, another EMT and I were dispatched to the local hospital to transport a patient to a hospital in Great Falls, where she could receive care by a neurosurgeon.

The patient had been found unconscious that morning in the alley behind the Moose Bar. She had been severely beaten. Both of her eyes were deeply blackened—a condition informally referred to by medical personnel as "raccoon eyes." This presentation suggested she may have sustained a serious head injury.

Just thirty miles shy of Great Falls, as we approached the little town of Cascade, I noticed that the ambulance gasoline gauge indicated our gas tank was almost dead empty. In our haste to begin our trip, I failed to check the gas gauge.

I drove into Cascade in the hopes we could buy gas there. Being Sunday, the only thing open for business was a local bar. I ran into the bar, which was full of patrons, and explained our dire situation and asked if anyone could sell us some gas. A fellow climbed off his bar stool and said he had a can of gas in his garage, which was located just across the train tracks from the bar.

We drove over to the man's garage and he brought out a five-gallon can and proceeded to pour the contents into our gas tank. The gas in the can was about half empty when he said, "Oh, by the way, this is outboard motor mix, but I think it will get you to Great Falls."

We paid the gentleman for the fuel and continued on our trip, black exhaust blowing out behind us as we made our way into Great Falls.

Unfortunately, we later heard that the woman had died sixteen hours after we'd delivered her to the hospital.

Buckle Up!

In the early 1980s I was dispatched as a volunteer ambulance EMT. We left Dillon, Montana, early on a winter afternoon, headed for a vehicle accident in the vicinity of the High Bridge. The High Bridge crosses the Beaverhead River on I-15 about fifteen miles south of Dillon.

A woman driver's car spun off the iced-over bridge deck. Her car rolled to the bottom of the slope below the bridge. The woman was ejected from her car. She was seriously injured.

Highway Patrolman Harold Forsman was on the scene when we arrived. As we were picking up the woman to load her in the ambulance, we heard another vehicle crash above us. That other vehicle spun off the bridge, rolled over once in mid-air, and landed upright about fifty feet from us! We could see the woman in the driver's seat swaying side to side in her car seat as the car suspension system settled town.

The woman was buckled up. She was uninjured!

To me one of the greatest incentives to buckle up is looking outside the window and seeing mile after mile of barb wire fences paralleling the highways and county roads in Montana.

One evening we responded to a vehicle accident on a highway north of Dillon. The driver failed to negotiate the curve at the bottom of Apex Hill, located about fifteen miles north of Dillon. He wrecked, and was ejected from his car. He was sieved through a barbed wire fence.

It was not a pretty sight.

Crushed

Early in the mid-1980s Sheriff Rick Later and I, in the Beaverhead Ambulance, responded to a truck accident about fifteen miles north of Dillon, Montana. The accident occurred on the highway to Twin Bridges, where an irrigation canal crosses under the highway.

During the night a large semi-truck hauling wheat south from Great Falls had drifted off the highway, sailed over the canal, and speared into the far bank. On impact, fifty tons of wheat shot forward, crushing the cab. The impact was so great that the front axle steering shaft was shoved back into the sleeper. Speculation has it that the truck driver must have fallen asleep. The driver was crushed to death. Highway Patrolman Harold Forsman was on the scene directing the early morning traffic.

Our task was to remove the truck driver's badly crushed body from the truck cab. There we were, struggling in knee-deep wheat, trying to extricate the body using the forty-five-pound jaws of life tool. The task was frustrated by the fiberglass cab closing back in every time we tried to reposition the tool.

We were finally ready to remove the body when I happened to look over my shoulder and see a woman standing on the road with her young daughter watching us. I called a pause to our efforts and walked up to the woman. I advised her that it was not a good idea for her young daughter to witness what we were about to remove from the cab. The woman and her daughter left.

I will never forget that grisly scene.

Burns

During my fifteen years as a volunteer EMT in Dillon, Montana, I served on the local ambulance, the ski patrol, and with the local search & rescue. I responded to emergencies involving victims of car and truck accidents, gun shots, a stabbing, drownings, carbon monoxide asphyxiations, heart attacks, suicides, a railroad accident, a sawmill accident, an airplane crash, a stroke, backcountry accidents, rodeo accidents, ranch accidents, ski accidents, violent beatings, broken hips, and deaths.

In my experience, I consider burns as the worst trauma.

One evening John Poundstone and I were asked to transport a burn patient to Butte. The woman was horribly burned, a victim of smoking in bed. John was the patient's attendant.

During the hour-long trip, the ambulance filled with the odor of burned flesh. Halfway to Butte, John asked me what he should do if the patient stopped breathing. I responded, "Bag her!" John said he was afraid that, if he applied the resuscitation bag, her face would slide off!

After delivering the patient to St. James Hospital in Butte, we returned to Dillon. As we drove home, the odor of burned flesh had totally permeated our clothing and the ambulance interior.

Upon arriving home in the wee hours of the morning, I deposited my smelly clothing in the laundry hamper. Then I showered and applied liberal amounts of underarm deodorant, followed by brushing my teeth, shaving, and splashing liberal amounts of aftershave lotion onto my face.

Finally, I crawled into bed, convinced that I would be free of the odor of burned flesh. But then, I belched just as I was falling asleep! The odor of burning flesh returned.

The patient died in the Houston burn center.

Sawed

One day in the early 1990s, I was in the break room in the Beaverhead National Forest supervisor's office when the cartographic technician walked in. He looked at me and said, "Swede, you don't remember me, do you?" When I replied I did not, he stated, "You picked me up one night at the Stoltze sawmill." I failed to recognize Don Rice because he'd grown a beard.

Around 10:00 p.m. on April 24th, 1974, as a volunteer EMT, I was dispatched along with an ambulance attendant to the Stoltze sawmill seven miles south of Dillon, Montana. Don was employed at the sawmill at that time. He was helping the sawyer clear an obstruction in the area of the twin vertical band saws. As he was exiting the area next to the saws, he slipped on some sawdust and fell backwards towards one of the rotating band saws. His left arm fell over the guard and his upper left arm was sliced open to the bone. Don, holding his injured arm, stumbled into the file room.

When our ambulance crew arrived at the sawmill file room, most of the night shift workers were in the file room with Don. (One man was losing his lunch over in a corner.) The shift foreman was applying a pressure point on the arm to stop the bleeding. That foreman most likely saved Don's life!

After applying a pressure bandage and splint to Don's arm, we transported him to the hospital in Dillon. After a quick examination by a physician, we were instructed to transport Don to the hospital in Butte.

After recuperating from his injury, Don returned to work at the sawmill. Don regained most of the function in his injured arm, but he continued to have some numbness in the outer edge of his left hand.

After the sawmill closed, Don knocked around doing odd jobs, but eventually he went to work for the Forest Service. His prior military service as a U.S. Air Force navigator made him a perfect fit to become the Beaverhead National Forest cartographic technician.

Reflection

The impact of vehicle on vehicle, and the result on the occupants, sometimes presents a scene that shocks the most seasoned first responders.

One weekend evening another ambulance EMT and I responded to a vehicle accident just north of Dillon, Montana. A father and his son were exiting the parking lot of a bar and restaurant when the side of their vehicle was slammed into by an oncoming vehicle.

When we arrived on scene, the place was bedlam. The crowd in the restaurant had emptied out and was milling about the accident scene. A highway patrolman was trying to control the chaotic situation. He appeared shook.

I entered the driver's side of the father's car to examine him. He was sitting with his head titled back, his mouth and eyes wide open. The small particles of glass stuck to his eyeballs reflected the light from my flashlight. (It suggested to me he hadn't even had time to blink!) It was obvious to me he was deceased.

The boy's symptoms suggested to me he had a devastating brain injury. He died shortly after we delivered him to the hospital in Dillon.

A couple of weeks later an attorney visited me at my home. He was representing the family of the deceased and requested a copy of the ambulance report. I informed him he would have to subpoena it. He returned later with the subpoena, whereupon I gave him a copy of the ambulance report.

He then asked me if the father was still alive when I arrived on scene. (I suspect the attorney was trying to establish pain and suffering, which could result in a larger cash settlement.)

I told the attorney I was not qualified to declare a person deceased. However, I informed the attorney that the father had no detectable carotid pulse or signs of respiration. His pupils were dilated (with glass particles stuck to his eyeballs), and he was cyanotic (blue) around his nostrils and lips. However, I repeated that I was not qualified to declare him deceased.

The attorney left. I suspect he didn't want me as a court witness.

Instinct

A family pet's animal instinct can complicate a first responder's ambulance call.

Early one morning in the 1970s, two of us ambulance EMTs were dispatched to a local ranch.

An elderly couple had consumed a large amount of alcohol before going to bed. During the night the wife, heavily inebriated, had fallen out of bed and hit her nose on the floor and bled out. (According to her husband, she had a history of high blood pressure.)

I knelt down to examine the wife. Her pupils were widely dilated, and there was cyanosis (blue color) about her nostrils and lips. I detected no pulse in her carotid and there were no visible signs of respiration. The husband, reeking of alcohol, stood over me with clenched fists and asked:

"Is she dead?" I responded, "I think so." He angrily replied, "YOU THINK SO?" and demanded: "IS SHE, OR ISN'T SHE?" I replied, "Yes, she's gone."

The husband started sobbing, so I stood up and backed him up against a wall to comfort him.

As I was attempting to comfort him, he was looking over my shoulder, viewing his deceased wife. After a few moments, he started going ballistic on me and was pointing to his wife. I looked over my shoulder and saw their house cat was lapping up his wife's blood!

I shooed the cat out of the bedroom and closed the door!

I called the county coroner and explained the situation to him. He instructed us to transport her to the local funeral home. We loaded up the woman and left. We were mighty glad to conclude that ambulance call!

Tib-Fib

In January 1974, I was working as a volunteer ski patrolman on the Maverick Mountain Ski Area. The ski area is located about thirty-four miles due northwest of Dillon, Montana.

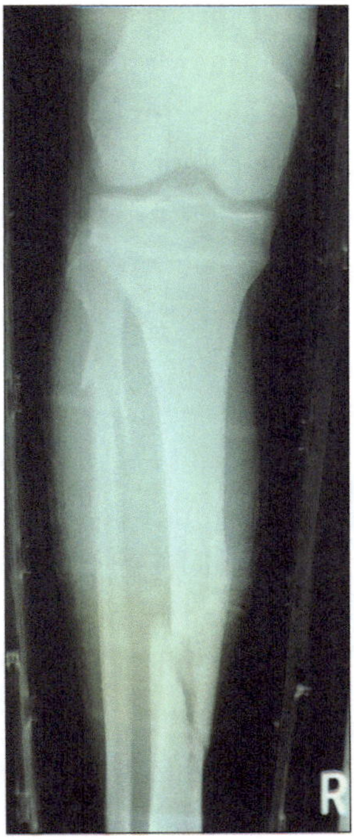

Skier's X-ray

About mid-afternoon, I received a report of an injured skier on the Ridge Run ski trail. Arriving at the accident scene, I discovered that a skier had injured his right leg when he landed hard after launching himself off a temporary ski jump. His symptoms indicated he had badly fractured his right leg.

After carefully removing the skier's skis and splinting his leg, I loaded him onto a sled and transported him to the bottom of the ski hill. Several ski patrolmen helped me load the skier into someone's private vehicle. Friends then transported the injured skier to the hospital in Dillon.

Following behind them in my own vehicle, I visited the injured skier at the hospital in Dillon. An X-ray revealed the skier had fractured his tibia (the large shin bone) and his fibula (the smaller adjacent leg bone). The attending physician referred the skier to Dr. Ron Losee, an orthopedic surgeon in Ennis, Montana.

Then by ambulance, I transported the injured skier and his X-ray to the Ennis Hospital. After viewing the X-ray, Dr. Losee complimented me on the care I had given the skier. He stated that, because the splint was so well applied, it had stabilized the fracture, and there would be no need for surgery.

Dr. Losee asked me to stay and help him to prepare the skier's leg for traction. Using a hand crank drill, Dr. Losee drilled a hole through the calcaneus (heel bone) so he could run a stiff wire through it to provide a point of attachment for the traction device.

The skier was laid up in traction for many weeks to allow the bones to completely heal. But, thankfully, he never required surgery because of the properly applied splint!

Closed Reduction

In the 1970s I was a volunteer ski patrolman at the Bridger Bowl Ski Area, located near Bozeman, Montana.

One Saturday night, the ski area received about a foot of new snow. Shortly after the ski area opened on Sunday, I responded to an injured skier on one of the ski runs. Arriving with a rescue sled at the injured skier, I discovered the injured skier was one of our ski patrolmen!

National ski patrolman appointment badge

The ski patrolman's injured leg was buried in the deep snow. I dug down to the patrolman's injured leg, and I saw that he had suffered a badly distorted lower leg fracture. His lower leg was bent sideways at mid-shaft, and it was rotated such that the toe of his ski boot was pointing to the right. The patrolman was in agonizing pain.

I carefully removed the patrolman's skis and informed him I would have to straighten his leg so I could splint it. Cradling the boot in my hands, and exerting slight tension, I began to straighten the leg. I carefully, VERY CAREFULLY (like porcupines make love), slowly rotated and straightened his injured leg, carefully lining up his big toe with his patella (kneecap).

As I was straightening his leg, he suddenly exclaimed, "Oh, the blood, the blood!" Alarmed, I thought I was dealing with an open leg fracture! I was relieved to find out his exclamation was one of pain relief as the blood to the lower part of his injured leg, which had been pinched off by the distortion, resumed flowing.

With assistance from other patrolmen, I carefully splinted his injured leg. We then loaded him into the rescue sled, and I transported him downhill to the ski patrol room at the lodge. Friends loaded him into a vehicle and transported him to the hospital in Bozeman.

The next weekend I was approached by the ski patrol medical advisor (a physician). He informed me that at the hospital the injured patrolman was diagnosed with a closed reduction fracture that did not require surgery! He asked me, "How did you do it?" In jest, I grinned and said, "Oh, I just lined up the leg with the crease in the ski pant." I then went on to explain to him how I did it. The physician shook his head and mumbled, "Amazing!"

Dislocated Hip

In February 2024, there a was skier fatality at the Discovery Ski Area in Montana. The skier ran into a tree. This reminded me of a similar accident that occurred at the Maverick Mountain Ski Area in the early 1980s, when I was the ski patrol leader.

Near closing time at the ski area, a local Dillon girl skied into a tree. One of her knees impacted the tree, which dislocated her hip.

The road from Highway 278 to the ski area was not paved at the time and was rapidly thawing during spring breakup. I figured that a ground transport over the entire length of that rough dirt road might exacerbate the injury and cause the girl great pain. I requested that a helicopter pick up the girl at Polaris, the nearest decent helicopter landing area.

We transported the girl by car to Polaris. When the helicopter landed near the Polaris Bar, everyone in the bar came out to watch the patient transfer. Along with the crowd, out dashed a dog!

The presence of that dog really concerned me! There have been instances where the high whine of a helicopter turbine engine has excited a nearby dog. I'd learned that in one case, the dog jumped up and tried to bite the tail rotor! If the dog touched the tail rotor, the tail rotor would probably injure or kill the dog, and the impact could also damage the tail rotor and disable the helicopter. We didn't need that!

I had someone in the crowd of onlookers restrain the dog, and we loaded the girl into the helicopter.

The girl was transported to the hospital in Butte.

Camero

One night in April 1970, I was dispatched as a volunteer EMT with the Beaverhead Ambulance Service to a wreck on "Deadman Curve," north of Dillon, Montana. "Deadman Curve" is at the bottom of a hill on the Old Highway 91 North, about four miles south of Glen, Montana.

Montana Highway Patrolman Harold Forsman was driving north on the highway when a blue Camaro flashed by him. Harold turned on his emergency lights and started pursuing the speeding car.

The new 1969 Camaro crashed at the bottom of "Deadman Curve," resting on its roof, up against a barbed wire fence. He found the driver and his passenger, both high school kids, hanging upside down in the car, suspended by their lap belts.

Upon our arrival in the ambulance, Harold informed me that as the car passed by him, its interior light came on momentarily. The driver of the Camaro told Harold that, as he turned on the interior light, he told his passenger, "Holy s**t! We just passed by a highway patrolman! Buckle up! We're going to outrace him."

The new Camaro had a hood with racing pins. The hood was lying out in the nearby field!

It's fortunate that those kids were buckled up! Had they been ejected from their car, they may have been sieved through that barbed wire fence.

The passenger suffered a compression fracture of his back.

Wooley Bugger

About thirty years ago I was returning to Dillon, Montana. I was driving north in my Bronco on the east frontage road, south of Dillon. Just past the sawmill I was waved down by Bill Jappe, who had exited his pickup truck.

As Bill approached me, I could see he had a large Wooley Bugger fishing hook embedded in the skin of his neck, just above the carotid artery. (A Wooley Bugger is a popular fishing fly used during the salmon fly hatch on local rivers.)

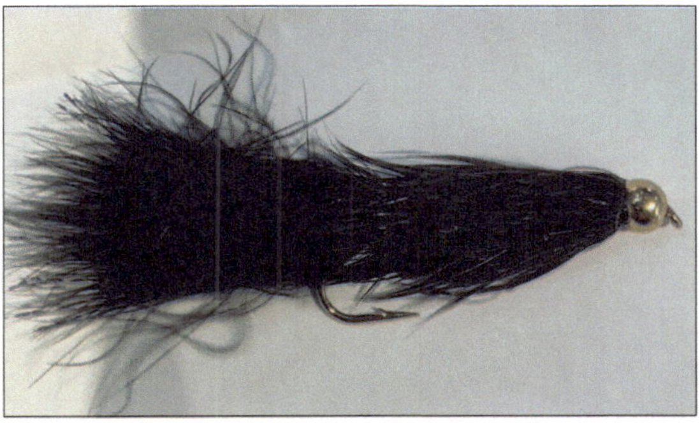

Wooley Bugger

Bill asked me if I could remove the hook.

I retrieved a pair of wire cutters from my truck tool kit, then proceeded to rotate the hook out so as to expose the barb near the tip. After clipping off the barb, I then rotated the hook back out of his skin.

Bill thanked me and went on his way.

Chapter Ten

OTHER STORIES

Horse Muffins

IN 1966, my wife MaryAnn and I backpacked into Green Lake for an overnight stay. Green Lake is located southwest of Melrose, Montana, in the East Pioneer Mountains.

Our approach to the east shore of Green Lake entailed a difficult scramble downhill and over a field of large boulders. Upon reaching the lake shore, it was an easy walk north along the lake shore to the inlet.

Pika. PHOTO COURTESY JACK KIRKLEY

The inlet is surrounded by a small, smooth, flat area. An ideal camping spot!

After setting up our tent to the bleating calls from numerous pikas, I pulled a plastic bread sack out of the bottom compartment of my Kelty backpack. In response to MaryAnn's inquiry as to what was in the sack, I responded, "Horse turds." I told her it was my intent to deposit the dry horse turds by the inlet and let the next visitor try to figure out how a horse managed to get into the area.

Three Shots for a Dime

It has been my privilege to reside in Dillon, Montana, for over fifty-five years. I served for a dozen years as a volunteer in city government. Dillon is a small agricultural and college town with a population of around 4,500 people. I think I know it well.

My perception is that occasionally a source of excitement in Dillon involves the wrong bars, or the wrong beds.

The Moose Bar

One evening in 1968, right at closing time, a well-sloshed customer put a dime in the jukebox.

The bartender came around from behind the bar and pulled the plug on the jukebox and informed the customer it was closing time and ordered him to leave. The bartender then returned to his side of the bar to close the cash register, whereupon the customer became very angry. The bartender placed a dime on the bar and told the customer to pick up the dime and get out. The customer climbed over the bar and smacked the bartender alongside his head. A vicious fight ensued, and during the fight the bartender broke away from the customer and retrieved a .38 special revolver. The bartender then fired the revolver three times, killing the customer.

At trial, the bartender pleaded self-defense. He was found guilty of a wrongful death and sentenced to ten years, with five suspended, in the state penitentiary at Deer Lodge.[1]

A joke got around town that the best place in town to buy a drink was at the Moose Bar, because you could get three shots for a dime!

Mooning the Tire

In the early 1980s my wife MaryAnn and I were returning home from a day ski patrolling at the Bridger Bowl Ski Area, which is near Bozeman, Montana. In the dark, between Bozeman and Belgrade, we came upon a car pulled over to the side of the interstate. A couple was hunkered down near the right-side rear tire. MaryAnn suggested we stop and offer assistance to the couple, who we suspected might be tending to a flat tire. Our intent was to at least offer them the benefit of our headlights.

After parking my car, and still wearing my ski patrol parka, I approached the couple. The husband, who was shielding his wife from the view from approaching traffic, was laughing. His wife was emitting a mixture of screeching and laughing. Her pants were down around her knees as she was relieving herself.

I said to myself, "Oops!" and quickly returned to my car. So much for good intentions!

Burning Permit

I called the county on 10/17/23 and notified them that I turn ninety on November 1st, and asked, "Do I need a Burning Permit before I light the candles on my birthday cake?"

The response was, "Keep it in a confined space."

Stirrups

Jay Bertino, a former smokejumper and college classmate of mine, related the following story to me.

[1] Ref: *Google State vs Steve Logan*

Gracie's

One day he was in Gracie's second-hand store in Dillon, Montana. While looking around the store, a pickup truck pulled up to the store. When the driver got out, Jay could see a ranch brand painted on the side of the door. The driver was a HUGE, angry-looking cowboy.

The cowboy walked through the store. He continued down the stairs located in the back of the store. The stairs led to the store basement. The next thing Jay heard was the cowboy ascending the stairs, saddle stirrups thumping against the steps.

The cowboy left the store carrying the custom saddle. Jay noticed that the back of the saddle cantle had the same brand as that displayed on the door of the truck. The cowboy placed the saddle into the bed of the pickup and drove off.

No one in the store said a word. Speculation has it that a friend of the cowboy recognized the stolen saddle in the store's basement and notified the cowboy.

Holy Water

Some years ago I noticed that our local funeral home owner was limping. When I inquired as to what caused his limp, he responded that he had fallen into a grave. When I expressed some sympathy, he said, "That happens," and related the following incident that occurred at a funeral.

He was attending a graveside funeral service at a nearby town. It had rained heavily the previous night. The coffin was placed on the lowering mechanism above the open grave. As the priest (not the funeral home owner) approached the coffin to sprinkle holy water on it, the rain-soaked edge of the pit sloughed off and the priest slid into the grave.

There he was, under the coffin, peering up at the grieving and shocked family and guests, who were trying to keep their composure.

Water Rights

From 2008 to 2017, I worked part time for an attorney in Dillon who had rancher clients. My task was to travel to ranches to correct the location descriptions on Water Right Abstracts. The Abstracts described the location of points of diversion, such as headgates and dams. These ranches were located in the Big Hole and Beaverhead Valleys in Montana.

Tom Glennon standing next to a headgate on the Big Hole River

Many of these water rights were filed in the late eighteen or early nineteen hundreds. I suspect there were no accurate maps in existence then.

I would obtain the accurate location coordinates with my GPS receiver and correct the location description by downloading the coordinates onto my computer map program. The correct location description had to be described down to the nearest ten acres. The corrected Water Right Abstracts and accompanying maps were then submitted to the Montana Water Rights Bureau, who would then issue the rancher a corrected Abstract.

Townships (thirty-six square miles) are described using township and range numbers. Within the townships are thirty-six numbered sections, each one mile square.

The location descriptions of two of the points of diversion were six miles off! One (a dam) had the wrong township number listed on the Abstract, and the other (a head gate) had the wrong range number listed on the Abstract. One section listed no head gates in it. It had ten, but they had been marked as existing in an adjoining section. Many of the location descriptions were a mile off.

The most satisfying part of this work was that I got to meet some very nice ranchers and visit some ground that was new to me.

In the West, there is a saying about water: "Whiskey is for drinking, water is for fighting."

Butte Pride

A few years ago, I went to our local hospital here in Dillon, Montana, to get some lab work done for my annual physical.

There was a beautiful receptionist checking me in. I remarked to her how gorgeous she was and asked her where she was from. She replied, "Butte." Then I remarked, "I guess that makes you a Buttetoid."

She replied, "Yes, and proud of it." On the back of her left hand, behind the thumb and forefinger, was a tattoo of a mining head frame.

Mining headframe in Butte.
PHOTO COURTESY SILKY/SHUTTERSTOCK

This was the best example of Butte pride I ever saw.

Place Names

Names are assigned to topographic features by the USGS Board on Topographic Names. What follows is a sample of topographic feature names and how they were determined.

Features named after individuals: The current policy is that a feature cannot be named after an individual until the person has been deceased for at least fifteen years. Public comment is solicited on the proposed name.

Bloody Dick Creek: This creek is in Beaverhead County, Montana. Locals claim that an early homesteader who immigrated from England had Richard as his first name. Richard kept saying bloody this or bloody that. After a while he earned the nickname of Bloody Dick. His nick name was assigned to the creek.

Names of local ranches: Tash Peak, Harrison Peak, and Hirshey Peak in Beaverhead County are named after ranching families who homesteaded in the Grasshopper and Big Hole Valleys.

Lewis and Clark: there are numerous topographic features and some towns in the West with the names of the Lewis and Clark Expedition leaders. Homer Young's Peak: This peak, west of Jackson, Montana, was named after a Jackson native. I was informed that he was wounded in action near the end of WWI and died in a hospital of the flu epidemic.

Lakes named after daughters: Wayne Smetanka, who was a ranger on the Tofte Ranger District, Superior National Forest, Minnesota, informed me that an early surveyor named a chain of lakes on the Tofte Ranger District after his daughters: Grace, Alice, and Phoebe (known locally as The Lady Chain).

Lake named after a ranger's wife: Frank Fowler, who was the district ranger for the Powell Ranger District in Idaho, named a lake Alice, after his wife.

Shape: Crescent Lake, Long Lake, Teacup Lake and Deerhead Lake are in the East Pioneer Mountains. Needle Peak is in the Anaconda Pintler Wilderness Area. All are in the Beaverhead National Forest in southwest Montana.

Names changed: At times, the USGS changes the original name given to a topographic feature. In the East Pioneer Mountains, **Joaquin Lake** was changed to **Waukena Lake.** In the Bungalow Ranger District on the Clearwater National Forest, Idaho, **Wet Ass Creek** was changed to **Weitas Creek.**

Color: In the Gravelly Mountains, south of Ennis, Montana, two lakes are named Blue Lake. There is also a Black Butte.

Other: Cow Bone Lake, southwest of Jackson, Montana, was given that name because one winter a bunch of cattle fell through the ice on that lake. Their bones could be seen at the bottom of the lake for years afterward.

Fish and animal species: Rainbow Lake is located in the East Pioneers. Elk, Goose, and Otter Lakes are in the south end of the Gravelly Mountains.

Towards the end of my career in the Forest Service, Dan Svoboda, the forest soils scientist, suggested I name a topographic feature after me because I had been on the Beaverhead National Forest for over thirty years. I informed Dan of the policy that a feature could not be named after a person until that person was deceased for over fifteen years. Dan offered that if I did the paperwork, he would submit the proposal after I died.

Dutch Treat

In the summer of 1999, I was poking around the Northern Lights sporting goods store in Bozeman, Montana. I happened to notice that a store clerk was showing some topographic maps to a man and woman couple. To satisfy my curiosity I drifted over to the couple and listened to the conversation as they were examining a map. I noticed the couple spoke with a foreign accent.

When it appeared that the clerk had concluded his conversation, I introduced myself and inquired about the couple's country of origin. They said they were emergency room physicians from Holland and intended to rent a canoe and go canoeing on lakes in Yellowstone National Park. I informed them that I could recommend a secluded campsite and lakes to paddle a canoe on. They seemed interested, so I suggested to the clerk that he leave us alone so he could help other customers. (I didn't want to share my favorite area with him.)

I explained to the couple that my favorite canoeing and camping area was on Cliff and Wade Lakes, located about forty-five miles south of Ennis,

Montana. My favorite campsite was near the Cliff Lake inlet. The area is secluded because the shallow lake depth for one half mile north of the inlet does not accommodate motorboat access. They would awaken in the morning to the croaking from numerous Sandhill cranes. Elk, deer, and other wildlife could be viewed across the inlet from their campsite.

I suggested that on their return trip to Bozeman, they stop at the Grizzly Bar & Cafe and order an excellent steak dinner. The cafe is about ten miles north of their exit onto the highway. After determining which maps to purchase, they thanked me and gave me a Dutch ball-point pen that had windmill and Dutch flag fobs attached.

After returning to Holland they sent me a thank you card. In it they wrote: "Be Welcome! Dear Nils. We were happy enough to meet you at Northern Lights. Remember? You gave us excellent advice and we did a lot of canoeing on Wade Lake, Cliff Lake etc. Superb! Quiet and unbelievably beautiful. And of course we had a wonderful dinner at the Gizzley Bar. (Nice people over there and wonderful food.) So we like to thank you again for your comments. Greetings from Frans and Hendrika"

Postcard picture & pen

London Bridge

Names etched on the London Bridge Foundation.
PHOTO COURTESY MIKE MEHN

In January 2023, I received a text from Mike Mehn, a retired Montana game warden and good friend of mine. Attached was a photo of names, and a Big Red One Infantry Division symbol, scratched into the foundation of the London Bridge. The bridge is located in Lake Havasu City in Arizona. Mike had stopped at Lake Havasu City on his way to New Mexico. The name Mike was interested in finding was Wayne Fitzwater, now deceased. Wayne had retired as a Montana game warden in Dillon, Montana.

In 1968 Robert McCulloch purchased the bridge in London. He had it dismantled and shipped to Lake Havasu City. The reassembly was completed in 1971.

Wayne was a legend among Montana game wardens. He and I became good friends. Wayne was a good canoe operator, which was something he and I had in common—as well as a love of the outdoors. He and I would encounter each other occasionally in our travels in the outdoors. Following his retirement in 1978, after twenty-seven years as a game warden, Wayne authored a book titled *Where in the Hell Did You Come From?*

In World War II Wayne served as a sergeant in the Big Red One Division of the U.S. Army. In 1942 Wayne's outfit was staged in England waiting to be shipped to French North Africa. In August 1942, on a weekend pass, Wayne and a PFC Smith took a trip into London. Upon visiting the London Bridge, Wayne scratched his name and the name of PFC Smith, along with the Big Red One Division symbol, into the foundation. Today the names and symbol are barely legible.

Wayne suffered gunshot wounds to his chest, left side, and a serious left leg wound in the North African campaign. He recuperated in a hospital in England. Wayne passed away in 2018 at the age of ninety-nine.

His accomplishments and awards are listed on his headstone in the Dillon cemetery.

Wayne's headstone. PHOTO COURTESY SWEDE

PFD

In the spring of 1960, I was paddling my canoe alone on Lake Inez, which is one of the lakes in the Thompson River chain of lakes, west of Kalispell, Montana.

While on the lake, I noticed two Montana game wardens in a truck observing me through binoculars. I paddled over to the shore to socialize with them. The warden driving the truck appeared to be the older of the two. As I came close to the shore, the younger warden jumped out of the truck and ran down to approach me. With a grin, I said, "Howdy, there!" I had the canoe nosed against the shore, and I was maintaining that position with a slow one arm scull (sweeping motion) stroke on the outer side of the canoe.

The young warden inquired if I had a life jacket (or PFD—Personal Flotation Device). I responded, "Yes, it's in a sack in the middle of the canoe." The warden said, "Let me see it," and began to step into my canoe. Concerned that the warden could tip us over into the water, I quickly executed my one-arm sculling stroke in a different manner that moved the bow away from the shore. This left the warden with one foot hanging out over the water, nearly causing him to fall in!

The warden was embarrassed, and he lost his cool. He barked, "I ought to ticket you for not having that life jacket readily available!" I replied, "Mister, you don't step into a canoe without advance permission. It's a good chance you could roll us over into the water!"

The older warden called the young warden back to the truck, whereupon they drove away.

I surmised that the older warden was giving the young warden some rather stern advice.

The Missouri

In 1983, my wife MaryAnn and I decided to take our three children on a six-day canoe trip on the Missouri River. We planned to put in at Fort Benton, Montana, and take out at the Robinson Bridge (James Kipp Recreation Area), where Highway 191 crosses the river, 149 river miles southeast of Fort Benton.

Prior to our trip, MaryAnn obtained from the Bureau of Land Management (BLM) office in Fort Benton the appropriate maps of our planned float route and a list of local outfitters. We had also made arrangements for an outfitter to drive our Bronco and trailer to our takeout.

Our first night was spent camped on the Fort Benton tennis court. During the night a raging rain, hail, and lightning storm hit Fort Benton. MaryAnn took a photo from her tent of a lightning strike hitting the tennis court!

The next morning the river was rolling bankfull, carrying whole trees and other debris. We decided to postpone our trip for two weeks to allow the river level to drop.

Two weeks later, we decided to put in at Coal Banks, forty-one river miles below Fort Benton. Our trip would start at the beginning of that portion of the river which in 1976 had been designated by Congress as the Upper Missouri National Wild and Scenic River. Our take-out point was still the Robinson Bridge. The trip would last four days and cover 108 river miles.

Part of the trip was through a canyon that has spectacular rock formations, which includes Eye of the Needle, fifty-six miles downstream from

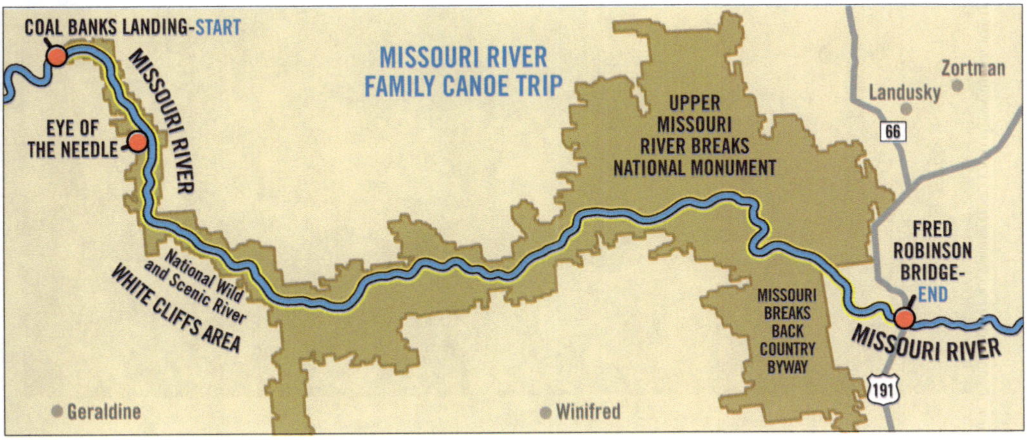

Eye of the needle (prior to 1997). PHOTO COURTESY BUREAU OF LAND MANAGEMENT

Remains of the eye of the needle. PHOTO COURTESY BUREAU OF LAND MANAGEMENT

Fort Benton. (These rock formations were described in the Lewis & Clark journals in their expedition up the Missouri River.) The Eye of the Needle collapsed in 1997. Two pillars of the formation remain.

We saw no game and caught no fish. The campgrounds, managed by the Montana Fish & Game Department, were in a pretty shabby condition. At one campground, my daughter was chased out of an outhouse containing a large hornets' nest. (The BLM has since taken over the management of these campgrounds.)

We ended our trip by spending the last night camped by the take-out point. The next morning, while waiting for the outfitter to deliver our Bronco and trailer, we watched a couple beach their boat and approach us. The woman was limping badly. She had tangled with the same wasp nest that my daughter encountered!

After the outfitter delivered our Bronco and trailer, we drove home. Our family adventure was time well spent, providing us memories for a lifetime!

Well War

In 1995, it came to my attention that the city of Dillon, Montana, had passed an ordinance that potable water well owners must connect to city water within ten years.

The city had just constructed a new water reservoir, and they were attempting to force well owners like me to contribute to paying off the construction cost.

At that time, my daughter Karin was enrolled in a constitutional law course in law school. I informed her of the city ordinance and that I had a water right on my well. (In Montana, a water right is considered a property right.) I also informed her the city was not

Water pump

willing to compensate me the $10,000 it would cost me to connect to city water. I questioned as to whether the city had followed proper due process, as we well owners had never been individually informed of the city proposal. Karin replied, "Oh, Dad, that's an illegal taking under the Fifth and Fourteenth Amendments to the United States Constitution!"

Following my conversation with Karin, I attended a City Council meeting. At that meeting I informed the Council that they could not force me off my well because I had a water right on it. Forcing me off my well would cost me $10,000 to connect to city water and would devalue my property.

The mayor replied that the issue has already been settled by the state Supreme Court. When I asked him the name of the case, he replied, "I'm not going to tell you."

I then inquired how many potable well owners were in the city. The mayor replied, "Only a couple of dozen." I would later find out that there were over fifty!

Replying to my inquiry, the Water Rights Bureau informed me that the appeal to the Supreme Court involved a couple from Ennis, Montana. They had been ordered to connect to city water in order to contribute to the cost of a new water reservoir having been constructed.

They lost their appeal because they never argued the issue of their property rights.

I called a meeting of well owners. Thirty-five attended, which included a state senator. At that meeting, I found out that many of the well owners mistakenly assumed that their Well Log was a water right. I explained to them that their Well Log was merely the well driller's documentation of their well's location, depth, flow rate, and type of use. A WELL LOG ITSELF DOES NOT CONFER A LEGAL WATER RIGHT!

I also informed the well owners that they could obtain a water right by obtaining a Water Right Application Form from the Clerk & Recorder's Office. After filling out the form, they could submit it to the Water Rights Bureau and obtain a Water Right.

The attendees signed a letter of complaint to the city. One paragraph in the letter began by stating, "Your attention is invited to the Fifth and Fourteenth Amendments to the United States Constitution."

A compromise was offered by the city. The city insisted that we well owners would derive improved fire protection from the new reservoir. City water users were charged a $10.18 monthly construction fee for the new reservoir. We well owners would be charged only half, or $5.09 monthly. But, best of all, the compromise included the agreement that our wells would be grandfathered in and that we would not be required to tie into the city's water supply. We accepted the compromise.

Later I was informed by the Clerk & Recorder's office that they received an inquiry from the Water Rights Bureau. They wanted to know why they were receiving so many Water Rights Applications from Dillon!

(This story appeared on the front page of the December 29th, 1995, issue of the *Montana Standard.*)

Too Fat to Fly

In March 1995, I was driving out to our local rifle range when I spotted a Golden Eagle in the middle of Ten Mile Road. The eagle was unable to fly.

I suspected that the eagle had either been hit by a vehicle or collided with a power line. With some assistance, I managed to capture the eagle. I brought it to the Dillon Small Animal Hospital for examination by veterinarian Andrea Simonsen. Dr. Simonsen had developed an interest in birds.

Swede and Andrea about to release the eagle.
PHOTO COURTESY PERRY BACKUS

After examining the eagle, Andrea determined it probably could not fly because it had recently gorged on too much food. At this time of spring, there should be plenty of emerging young ground squirrels and cow afterbirth available for eagles to feast on.

Andrea kept the eagle overnight. The next day, in the company of Peri Backus (a *Montana Standard*

Andrea releasing the eagle. PHOTO COURTESY PERRY BACKUS

reporter) and me, Andrea released the eagle at the location where I'd captured it.

Despite having had an opportunity overnight to digest its food, the eagle still struggled to fly off.

(This story appeared on the front page of the March 16th, 1995, issue of the *Montana Standard.*)

Location Poster

In mid-January 2024, Billy Pierce, a resident of Dillon, Montana, visited me at my home in Dillon. He had been splitting firewood and noticed a metal Forest Service location poster that had been nailed on a tree that had become a piece of his firewood. He noticed the initials NT on the tag. He figured it stood for Nils Troedsson, and he thought, "Hey, I know this guy 'Swede' Troedsson!"

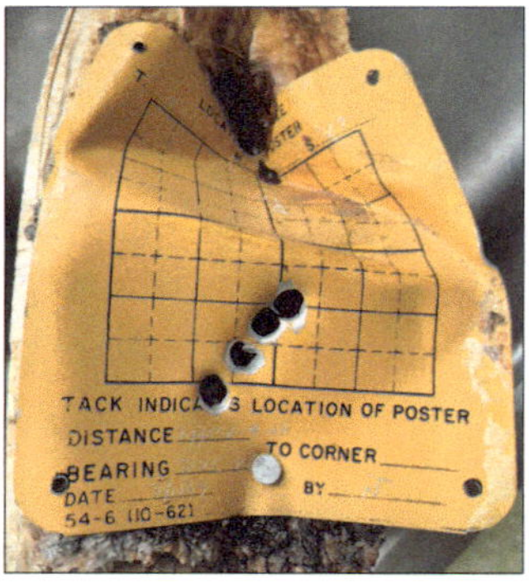

Location poster

He presented me with the damaged poster mounted on the piece of lodge pole pine. The information still visible scratched on the tag follows:

> **T (Township)—5 S (south)**
> **R (Range) obliterated**
> **S (section) 19**
> **Distance (to the nearest surveyed corner) 4 ch. (chains—264 feet)**
> **Bearing—Due W (west)**
> **Date (posted)—9/1/69)**
> **By NT**

I had enough information that I was able to surmise it was located on the west side of the Bull Creek Road no. 7485 and refers to the nearby surveyed quarter-section corner. I remember posting this tag fifty-four years ago to protect the corner during logging operations!

Bull Creek is about thirty-two miles northwest of Dillon and drains into Governor Creek, which eventually drains into the Big Hole River.

One might be impressed with the tight grouping of the bullet holes. My guess is that this slob visitor to the National Forest was only thirty feet away. My hope during my career with the Forest Service was to catch someone destroying government property so I could report them. Some folks just have no manners.

Phantom 309

At dusk one winter evening in the early 70s, I was returning to Dillon from Helena, Montana. It was snowing lightly. Snow skittered lazily across Highway 41 in front of me. Between Twin Bridges and Dillon, I was listening to Red Sovine's song "Phantom 309" on KOMA, an Oklahoma City radio station. That song is about a truck driver who lost his life as he swerved off the road in order to avoid hitting a bus full of kids.

In my rear-view mirror, I saw the headlights of an approaching semi-truck. As the semi roared past me, I caught a glimpse of the Bull Dog ornament perched on the hood of his Mack truck.

Once the truck was ahead of me, I got on my CB radio and said, "Howdy, 18-wheeler. The Meat Man here." The truck driver immediately replied, "Back to you, Meat Man, Phantom 309 here."

I replied, "As we speak, they are playing your song on KOMA!"

The truck driver replied, "I'm listening to it!"

In nothing flat, he was clean out of sight!

How cool was that?

(You can Google "Phantom 309." It's an-all time classic, first released in 1967.)

Rewards

Some years ago, my girlfriend at the time and I drove in from Red Lodge to shop in Billings, Montana. One of our stops was at a Cabela's store. In front of the store, large numbers of side-by-side four-wheelers and boats were lined up.

I decided to visit the GPS receiver counter. While there I noticed four large, rough-looking men at the gun counter. I asked the GPS salesman who those men were at the gun counter. He replied they were oil workers from "the Patch" (North Dakota oil fields).

He went on to tell me that there were two brothers in Williston, North Dakota, that owned a large trucking company. They would haul water to the oil drill sites. He said that they would charge EVERYTHING on their Cabela's credit card. In just a year's time they would earn over $10,000 in credit card rewards!

One of the brothers had just left the store with a $2,000 Swarovski spotting scope.

The Galloping Swede

In the early twenties my dad and his two brothers immigrated to America from Sweden. All earned a college education. One became a physician, one became an architect, and my dad worked for the Chase Manhattan Bank in New York City in foreign credit for forty years.

Dad always wanted to visit Montana. So, in 1957, while I was a college student in Missoula, Montana, I accepted a summer job with the USDA Forest

Service in Skykomish, Washington. The plan was that Dad would travel on the train from New York to Montana. I would drive in my Nash Rambler from Missoula to meet Dad in Miles City, Montana. He would ride with me across Montana to Washington, where I would start my summer employment. In Seattle he would board a train for the return trip to New York City.

Our first day in Miles City, we attended the exciting annual Bucking Horse Sale! The second day, we stayed overnight in a motel in Helena. The next morning, we ate breakfast in a local cafe.

At the cafe counter sat a large man eating his breakfast. His heavy Swedish accent caught my dad's attention. Dad struck up a conversation in Swedish with the man. The man stated he was Hugo Aronson, the governor of Montana! Hugo went on to explain that he left the poverty in Sweden and immigrated to America in 1911. The first time he set foot in Montana was when he was kicked off a freight train!

Hugo would go on to stay in Montana and make his fortune establishing a trucking company that serviced the oil fields in Toole County, Montana. He was known as "The Galloping Swede." Hugo invented a method to move oil drilling platforms without having to dismantle them.

Hugo Aronson, 1891–1978. PHOTO COURTESY STATE OF MONTANA

Hugo also served in the Montana legislature and would later serve as a two-term governor from 1953 to 1961.

Only in America could you arrive someplace by being kicked off a freight train, and then stay to become the governor of that state! Hugo authored a book titled *The Galloping Swede.* It's a great story about Hugo's life.

Harrison Peak

The United States Board on Geographical Names, operating under the United States Secretary of the Interior as an agency within the U.S. Geological Survey, is responsible for approving the naming of topographical features.

The Board's policy is that a topographic feature cannot be named after an individual until that individual has been deceased for at least fifteen years. Public comment on the proposal must be solicited and must meet the approval of the public land management agency or the private land-owner of the area on which the topographic feature is located.

In early 1998, after retiring from the USDA Forest Service in 1994, I decided to propose naming a peak located on the Big Hole Divide after the Harrison ranching family. The peak is on the western edge of the Grasshopper Valley, approximately twenty-eight miles west-northwest of Dillon, Montana.

The feature would be named in honor of Marshall C. Harrison, who received a land patent in the Grasshopper Valley in 1896, and whose family has managed a livestock operation there ever since.

Comments on the proposal were solicited through official news releases by the Beaverhead-Deerlodge National Forest, and in newspaper articles in the *Montana Standard* and the *Dillon Tribune.* Twenty petitions were distributed throughout the local area.

There were 138 local residents who signed petitions in support of the proposal. Letters of support were received from Beaverhead County Sheriff Harold Forsman and State Senator Bill Tash. One letter of objection was received from a Butte resident who felt the peak should be named after a Native American.

Support was also expressed by the Beaverhead County Commissioners, the Montana Department of Natural Resources & Conservation, the USDA Forest Service, and the Montana State Board on Geographic Names.

In December 1998, the proposal was submitted to the Beaverhead-Deerlodge National Forest.

The Forest Service then forwarded it to the Region One Forest Service office in Missoula, who then forwarded it to the national office of the USDA Forest Service in Washington, D.C. Upon their approval, the Washington office submitted the proposal to the United States Board on Geographic Names.

In 2001 the Harrison Peak name proposal was approved by the U.S. Board on Geographic Names.

Later, Forest Soil Scientist Dan Svoboda suggested that I propose having a peak named after me because of my long-term tenure on the Beaverhead-Deerlodge National Forest. I informed Dan of the policy that a topographic feature cannot be named after an individual until after that individual has

Dr. Ron Loge & family at Harrison Peak. PHOTO COURTESY "SWEDE" TROEDSSON

been deceased for at least 15 years. Dan offered that, if I would do the paperwork, he would submit it 15 years after I died!

On July 4th, 2002, I accompanied Dr. Ron Loge and his family to Harrison Peak. While there, we installed a wooden sign with the name of the peak routed into it. I was proud to have been instrumental in the official naming of that peak.

Carnation Garden

Shortly after I retired from the USDA Forest Service in 1994, I kept accepting dispatches by the Montana DNRC (Department of Natural Resources & Conservation) as an air support group supervisor, which was considered to be a critical shortage category at that time.

That summer, I was dispatched to a state wildland fire on the Stillwater State Forest. The state forest headquarters is located in Olney, Montana, about fifteen miles northwest of Whitefish, Montana.

The first day I arrived on the fire, I visited the fire helibase, a temporary helicopter landing area which was located some distance east of the headquarters.

That evening, I attended the state lands fire overhead team meeting in Olney. I informed the team that there was quite a "carnation garden" (wads of toilet paper) growing around the helibase and recommended that porta potties be delivered to the helibase. It was my understanding that the helibase was located in a municipal watershed!

Those overhead were shocked! They were in the early stages of organizing logistics on the fire, and they hadn't even considered ordering porta potties for the helibase.

The next morning, when I returned to the helibase, four porta potties had to be quickly moved off of the helicopter operations landing area so we could start allowing the helicopter operations to begin that day!

Tattoo

Recently, in Dillon, Montana, I complimented a woman on her neck tattoo. She smiled and thanked me and pulled up one sleeve to show me a tattoo on that arm.

With an evil grin, she said, "And I've got one—" I interrupted her and said, "STOP RIGHT THERE!" (Go figure!)

Goodyear Snakes

Following a semi-truck too closely can lead to an unpleasant surprise.

At dusk in the early 1990's, my wife Pat and I were driving from Deerlodge to Dillon, MT. Upon entering the Interstate, we found ourselves behind a semi-truck. Behind this moving semi-truck there were sparks occasionally lighting up on the asphalt. The semi was hauling crushed cars. The sparks were being caused by metal debris hitting the pavement after falling off that load of crushed cars! This load did not have a safety net over the crushed cars.

Before I became fully aware of the source of the sparks, a piece of metal hit my windshield!

As the semi-truck continued on its way, I saw a highway patrolman engaged in a traffic stop on the other side of the Interstate. I stopped my car and ran across the Interstate to the patrol car and informed the patrolman of this situation. He immediately radioed ahead, relaying that information to a patrolman at a traffic stop further up the highway. That next patrolman gave chase, but before he could overtake that semi, HIS windshield was impacted by a piece of metal!

That semi-truck driver was cited for an unsafe load. When I caught up to him, I asked that truck driver to give me the name and telephone number of his company. However, I decided not to pursue the incident because the damage to my car's windshield was very slight.

Earlier this year (2024), I was complimenting my neighbor on her new car. She explained that she was forced to buy a new car because her previously owned car was totaled by a hood that flew off a pickup truck that was being transported by a semi-truck that was just in front of her. (Speculation has it that the pickup truck's hood was not latched).

Because of the heavy traffic right behind her, she dared not slam on her brakes. She could only watch as that airborne truck's hood slammed into her car's windshield. Fortunately, she was not injured. The truck driver was cited for an unsafe load (no net over the load.)

In the early 1980's I was returning from Wise River, MT to Dillon in a Forest Service truck. I was following a semi-truck. Just east of Dewey, I watched as a recap layer on one of his rear tires began to peel off. It was headed right towards me! I slammed on my truck's brakes and watched as about four feet of recap hit the asphalt about two feet in front of the hood of my truck! My vehicle was not damaged. (Some truckers refer to those lost recaps as "Goodyear snakes".)

Following a semi-truck too closely makes a truck driver nervous. They like to keep an eye on traffic following close behind them in case they have to make a sudden move. If you can't see either of the truck driver's outside rear view mirrors, then the driver cannot see you.

Partner

For the past ten years, my life has been blessed with a relationship with Debbie Mathis. She is a sweet and caring partner. Debbie is independent and unflappable. She is intelligent, a hard worker, has a quiet sense of pride, and maintains a positive and optimistic attitude. Her constant expression and demonstration of her love for me deepens my love for her.

ABOUT THE AUTHOR

"SWEDE" TROEDSSON was born and raised in the East. His early years in the Boy Scouts developed his love of the outdoors. Following high school, his first job with the USDA Forest Service began his love affair with Montana and the West.

Summer seasonal work with the Forest Service was interrupted by two years active duty in the U.S. Marine Corps. This service included a deployment to Korea.

Smokejumping while attending Montana State University (now called The University of Montana) introduced him to the diversity of the West and the excitement that comes with challenges presented in the outdoors.

After graduating from college with a degree in forestry, his employment as a forester eventually led him to Southwest Montana. The last thirty-one years of his career were spent on the Beaverhead National Forest. His main duties were preparing and administering timber sales. Other duties "as assigned" were coordinating motorized travel restrictions among nine public land and road management agencies, managing aviation resources, and being dispatched to wildland fire incidents from Florida to Alaska.

His volunteer work on the National Ski Patrol would lead him into volunteer emergency medical services (EMS), teaching emergency medical technicians, participating in volunteer ambulance work, and performing backcountry rescue. His certification as a private pilot, as well as his experience managing aviation resources in the Forest Service, enhanced his skills in EMS and backcountry rescue.

His love of hunting, fishing, canoeing, camping, and volunteer work with game wardens led him to other adventures.

Besides volunteer work, he found time to help his wife raise three children, introduce them to the outdoor recreational opportunities, and send them off to college. Following his retirement from the Forest Service, he was recruited by the University of Montana—Western to teach a course in Map, Compass, & GPS. It would be a satisfying seventeen-year experience.

He continues to reside in Dillon, Montana.

Debbie, Swede, & Harry

Addendum

FAVORITE RECIPES

RASPBERRY RHUBARB PIE

Pie Crust Supreme
(Makes three 9-inch crusts)

INGREDIENTS:

- 3 cups unbleached flour
- 1¼ cups Crisco shortening
- 1 tsp salt
- 1 whole egg
- 1 Tbsp apple cider vinegar
- 5½ Tbl cold water

FOR TOP CRUST GARNISH:

- 2 tsp milk
- 1 egg yolk *(the egg white is saved to be brushed onto the bottom crust prior to pouring in the filler)*
- 2 tsp sugar

Cut flour and shortening together until it resembles small pebbles.

Combine beaten egg, vinegar, water, and salt, and pour over flour mixture. Mix until blended and press into ball. Separate into 3 equal pieces, wrap, and chill for 1 hr. before rolling out bottom and top dough between sheets of wax paper. Use fresh wax paper for rolling out the upper crust. The dough rolls out easier if allowed to warm up to room temperature. (To facilitate positioning the bottom dough into the pie dish, remove the top layer of wax paper and center the upside-down pie dish on the dough.) Then slide one hand under the wax paper, and with the other hand holding the dish in place, turn the wax paper, dough, and plate over. Carefully remove the wax paper (using a knife edge to assist separating the dough from the wax paper). Trim the dough, allowing a ¼-inch over-hang. Brush the entire bottom crust with egg white.

After adding filler to bottom crust, top with 2 tsp butter, add top crust, trim, allowing a ¼-inch overlap, and crimp. Lightly brush top crust with mixture of milk and 1 egg yolk, and sprinkle with sugar. Cut steam vents. Leftover dough can be wrapped in Saran Wrap and frozen (good for up to 3 months—dough rolls out better after freezing and defrosting).

Raspberry/Rhubarb Pie Filler

Preheat oven to 425 degrees F.

INGREDIENTS:

- 1¾ lbs rhubarb stalks, cut into 1-inch pieces and cooked with ¾ cup sugar (start with ¼ inch water in bottom of pot—yields 3 cups cooked)
- 3 cu. (12 oz.)raspberries, mashed with ½ cu. sugar (yields 2 cu.)
- ½ cu. fast cooking tapioca
- 1 tsp salt

Bake pie for 40 min. After 15 min., cover edge with aluminum foil (held in place with round toothpicks). 10 min. prior to completion of the baking period, cover top crust with aluminum foil. After baking, let pie cool (filling sets up best if the baked pie is refrigerated for 4 hrs.) and serve with ice cream.

CHOCOLATE MOUSSE

Makes five servings

INGREDIENTS:

- 6 oz Baker's semi-sweet baking chocolate
- 3 eggs
- 1/8 cup sugar
- ½ Tbsp vanilla extract
- ½ cup heavy whipping cream

Melt over hot water: Baker's semi-sweet baking chocolate. Power mix egg yolks until thick and creamy. Add melted chocolate to whipped egg yolks and power mix entire mixture. To egg whites, add sugar and vanilla. With a wire whisk, in a power mixer, whip egg whites until fluffy and add to melted chocolate and egg yolks mix. Add heavy whipping cream. Power mix entire mixture, then pour into individual dessert cups or 5 oz Dixie Cups. Chill 2 hours or more. Serve with whipped cream.

COFFEE MOUSSE

Makes seven servings

INGREDIENTS:

- 30 large marshmallows
- 1 cup coffee
- 1 tsp Folgers Instant Coffee
- 1 cup heavy whipping cream

Melt marshmallows into coffee strengthened with instant coffee, whisking constantly. Refrigerate ½ hour to hour), or until just jelling. With a wire whisk attachment on a power mixer, whisk heavy whipping cream until fluffy. Hand whisk whipped cream into the mixture. Pour into 6 oz dessert cups or into 5 oz Dixie cups and chill.

(Goes great with Kahlua!)

RANGER RON'S SPAGHETTI SAUCE

Makes eight 1-cup servings

INGREDIENTS:

- Tbsp vegetable oil
- 1 diced medium-sized onion
- 1 lb burger
- 8 oz can "pieces & stems" mushrooms
- 1 heaping Tbsp minced garlic
- 1 heaping Tbsp sweet dried basil
- 1 heaping Tbsp spaghetti seasoning
- 2 24-oz jars commercial pasta sauce
- 1 golf ball size lump of brown sugar
- 2 Tbsp Kraft original barbecue sauce
- 3 shakes Tabasco sauce
- ½ tsp salt
- ¼ tsp course ground pepper
- ¼ cup apple cider vinegar

In a 12-inch frying pan, cover bottom with vegetable oil. Fry onion until translucent. Don't over fry. Break burger into small pieces and toss in with onions. Continue stirring burger and onions, breaking burger into smaller pieces until burger turns light brown. Add salt and pepper. Add mushrooms. Stir mushrooms into mixture. Add minced garlic to the mixture. Add basil and spaghetti seasoning. Now add commercial pasta sauce. Rinse each jar with about ½ to ¾ cup water and pour into mixture to thin slightly. Add Kraft original barbecue sauce. Then add 3 shakes of Tobasco hot sauce—not too much. More can be added later if desired. Add brown sugar and cider vinegar. More brown sugar and vinegar can be added for taste. Mix thoroughly and let mixture simmer and bubble for 1 to 1 ½ hours to blend all ingredients. Left over can be frozen in pint Ziploc bags (1 cup per bag).

BAKED TILAPIA

Preheat oven to 350 degrees F

Mix basting sauce. Coat bottom of baking dish with butter. Pat fillets dry with paper towels and place on the butter.

Spread sauce on top of fillets. Bake for 10 minutes, then increase heat to 400 degrees F and bake until fillets brown and sauce bubbles.

INGREDIENTS:

- Tilapia fillets
- 2 Tbsp butter

BASTING SAUCE (PER ½ LB FILET):

- 2 Tbsp mayonnaise
- ¼ cup grated Parmesan cheese
- 4–6 capers
- Dash of caper brine
- Sriracha hot chili sauce to taste

BOURBON BASTED SALMON

Place salmon skin side down in a shallow baking dish. Remove all bones. In a small bowl, combine all marinade ingredients. Pour over salmon and marinate in refrigerator at least 1 hour. Spray or coat grill with vegetable oil. Remove salmon from marinade (save the marinade). Sprinkle with lemon pepper. Grill salmon over hot coals (flesh side first), turning once until opaque throughout. While grilling the skin side, baste the grilled flesh side with reserved marinate during cooking.

INGREDIENTS:

- 1 lb salmon fillet
- lemon pepper

MARINADE:

- 3 Tbsp bourbon
- ¼ cup brown sugar
- 3 Tbsp green onion, chopped
- 2 Tbsp soy sauce
- 2 Tbsp vegetable oil

WINTER WILD RICE WITH DRIED CHERRIES[1]

Makes three servings

INGREDIENTS:

- 1 Tbsp butter
- ¼ cup chopped shallot
- 13 oz canned chicken broth
- ½ cup wild rice
- ¼ tsp dried thyme
- ¼ cup chopped hazelnuts
- 1/3 cup dried cherries
- 1 Tbsp fresh parsley, chopped

Melt butter in a medium saucepan over medium heat. Sauté shallot until soft but not brown (about 5 minutes). Add chicken stock. Increase heat to high and bring to a boil. Add rice and thyme, reduce heat to low, cover, and cook 40 minutes.

Meanwhile, toast hazelnuts on baking sheet for 8 minutes. While still warm, place nuts in a towel and rub together to remove as much of the dark brown husk as possible. Chop nuts coarsely.

Add nuts and cherries to rice, cover, and continue cooking 15 minutes or until rice is tender and until most of the stock has been absorbed. Rice should be glossy and moist.

Sprinkle with parsley and serve immediately.

HOLLANDAISE SAUCE

INGREDIENTS:

- 3 egg yolks
- 1½ Tbsp fresh strained lemon juice
- ¼ lb butter
- ¼ tsp paprika
- few flakes cayenne

Place 3 egg yolks in a double boiler. (In the absence of a double boiler, egg yolks can be placed in a small crock. The crock can be placed in a strainer and suspended over a pot of boiling water, making sure the water does not touch bottom of crock. Whisk egg yolks until they begin to thicken. Add 4 Tbsp of boiling water, 1 Tbsp at a time. Whisk the water into the egg yolks each time. Then whisk in warm lemon juice. Whisk egg yolks, water, and lemon juice until the mixture is creamy. While egg yolk

[1] Salmon and Wild Rice Recipes from Simply Classics by The Junior League of Seattle. Inclusion approved by info@usbookspublisher.com

mixture is getting creamy, in a microwave, melt butter in a cup. When egg yolk mixture has become creamy, remove crock from the boiling water and whisk in the melted butter. Whisk in paprika and a few flakes of cayenne.

If use is delayed, refrigerate. Prior to serving, microwave 30 seconds. Whisk before serving.

FLANK STEAK

Makes four servings

INGREDIENTS:

- 1¼–1½ lbs flank steak

MARINADE:

- ½ cup dry red wine
- ½ cup soy sauce
- 4 tsp minced garlic
- ¼ cup dried parsley flakes
- ¼ tsp course ground black pepper

Combine the marinade ingredients in a non-reactive bowl. Add the flank steak & coat it well with the marinade. Marinate the flank steak for about 8 hours, turning twice.

Remove from the marinate and pat dry. Charcoal grill the steak over high heat 3 inches from the heat for 4 minutes per side for medium rare meat. Remove to a cutting board and let rest for 10 minutes before slicing.

To serve, slice thinly on the diagonal and arrange on a board or platter.

BEEF OR ELK STROGANOFF

Preheat oven to 300 degrees F

INGREDIENTS:

- 1½ lbs trimmed meat
- 1½ cups all-purpose flour
- Salt & pepper
- 1½ Cu. (½ lb.) mushrooms sliced
- 14.5 oz. can beef broth
- 1 Tbsp tomato paste
- 3 Tbsp sour cream
- 4 Tbsp butter or light cooking oil
- ¾ Cu. onion, thinly sliced

Mix salt and pepper into flour. Cut meat into 3/4 inch cubes and dredge in seasoned flour.

Heat 2 Tbsp butter or light cooking oil in a large cast iron pan or Dutch oven. When butter or oil is foaming, but not smoking, add coated meat in batches and brown on all sides, cooking roughly 2 minutes per batch. Remove meat from pan.

Add more oil or butter. Then add onion. Saute 2 minutes until softened. Stir mushrooms. Cook 2 minutes. Stir in tomato paste or ½ cup tomato puree, beef broth, and pinch of salt & pepper.

Add meat to pan. Add enough water to cover meat. Bring to a boil. Cover with lid. Bake in oven 1½ hours.

Remove from oven. Stir in 3 Tbsp sour cream and 2 Tbsp butter.

Serve over egg noodles or mashed potatoes. Sprinkle with chopped parsley.

Serve with warm bread for sopping up the flavorful gravy afterward.